THE 13TH POWER

PERFORMING AT YOUR BEST ...IN SPORTS AND IN LIFE

Praise for ***The 13th Power***

"This is great material. Every coach should have this book."

—Jon Urbanchek, U.S. Olympic swim coach

"Being at your best in a sport is mainly about staying mentally focused and keeping your cool. *The 13th Power* teaches you how to do that."

—Darryl Swarts
Lacrosse goalie, MVP
University of Vermont

"*The 13th Power* provides a very clear and graphic presentation of what it takes to perform at one's best."

—Jeff McCullagh
McCullagh Creative, Advertising & Design

"Handling the pressure is what it takes to win. *The 13th Power* will teach you how to relax—control your nerves—and play at your best. Get it!"

—Dave Kendall
Kendall Academy
PGA: Director of Instruction

"As a lifelong sports enthusiast, and with a career in sales for over forty years, I've read a bundle of books on motivation and top performance. *The 13th Power* sums it all up. It's clear and concise—the best of the bunch."

—Tom McCarthy
The Villages, Florida

"As a former all-state high school middle distance runner, I wish I had been coached on this insightful approach for maximizing athletic talent. Currently, I am pursuing my dream of running a marathon and will undoubtedly use the techniques learned in *The 13th Power* to help me perform at my best."

—Christian Weder, graduate student,
Loyola University

"Great book! The breathing techniques and the overall method totally apply to what I do in teaching/coaching music performance. Playing an instrument is a sport too, as I tell my students, in that we use our bodies and minds to present a performance, with special exercises to isolate certain skills in advance. We hone the ability of our bodies to use our instruments to a point of mastery and transcendence for the highest expression of the music.

—Armena Marderosian, Suzuki Piano teacher
Teacher trainer for the Suzuki Association of the Armerica

"We have all been waiting for this. On the field, the shop floor, in the classroom or boardroom, it has always been about finding and mining our human capital. *The 13th Power* is a straightforward and concise book that provides us with the tools to help individuals and teams realize their potential."

—Michael J. McGinnis,
Human Resources Director
Orange County, North Carolina

THE 13TH POWER

PERFORMING AT YOUR BEST
...IN SPORTS AND IN LIFE

A. ALEX WORTMAN

POWERS PRESS
ANN ARBOR, MICHIGAN

Powers Press
1705 Wells Street
Ann Arbor, Michigan 48104
734-665-6580

Library of Congress Cataloging-in-Publication Data

Wortman, A. Alex., 1937-
The 13th power / A. Alex Wortman.
p. cm.
ISBN 0-923568-76-X
1. Physical education and training. 2. Performance.
I. Title: Thirteenth power. II. Title.
GV711.5.W67 2006
613.7'1019--dc22

2006007503

Printed in the United States of America

"Who but the self can be master of the self?"

Dhammapada

"One must raise the self by the self
And not let the self sink down."

Bhagavad-Gita

"Make the most of yourself,
for that is all there is of you."

Ralph Waldo Emerson

CONTENTS

Energy Cycle

A *successful act* is a well-managed
Energy Cycle
with a preparation phase,
an execution phase,
and a completion phase.

Self-Mastery is the integration of
twelve distinct energies.
It is your 13th power.

Beginning

> *"We would all like to be better performers at everything we do—better producers, leaders, organizers, homemakers, athletes, dancers, lovers. We would all like to read faster and write more coherently, think more clearly and sleep more soundly."*
>
> —Laurence E. Morehouse, *Maximum Performance*

What is the key to performing at one's best?

A certain shoe company provides a snazzy three-word response to that question—"Just do it." For most of us, however, the matter is a bit more complicated. But I'm not opposed to short answers—especially those that speak to our intuitions and encourage us to act. So this book presents its own succinct answer: Self-mastery—the 13th Power.

I've chosen images and metaphors of sports to illustrate this crucial component of optimal performance. Whether you are a fifty-year-old, out-of-shape amateur attempting a seven-foot winning putt at a small town family golf outing or a superstar professional stepping up to the plate at Yankee Stadium with the bases loaded and the game on the line, mastery of your energies is the key to performing at your best.

The 13th Power decodes the achievement process and the secrets of peak performers.

An individual act is the fundamental unit of any achievement and the driving force of an act is the *energy* of the performer. This book provides a detailed analysis of how a top performer effectively carries out an isolated act (such as stepping up to the plate and hitting a ball). A *successful act* is a well-managed *Energy Cycle* with a preparation phase, an execution phase, and a completion phase.

When you spontaneously and successfully take charge within those crucial moments of carrying out each phase of an individual *act*, you experience that right rhythm and flow and you perform with poise and confidence. And with each well-composed act that you produce, you strengthen your sense of Self-mastery.

By the time you finish reading *The 13th Power,* the three disciplines above—*preparation, execution, completion*—will be engrained in your brain. And as you fully master the *Energy Cycle*, the spontaneous use of your powers within each phase of the cycle will become your habitual way of doing things. It'll all happen unconsciously and instantaneously. You'll simply see where you want the ball to go and you'll take your swing. You'll have your act together. Indeed—you'll "Just do it."

As you acquire mastery of your self and of your energy cycles, your overall performance in sports and in life will improve dramatically.

1

Take Charge

> *"When you ride a horse, balance comes, not from freezing your legs to the saddle, but from learning to float with the movement of the horse as you ride. Each step is a dance, the rider's dance as well as the dance of the horse."*
>
> —Chogyam Trungpa, Writer, *Shambhala*

The seed for this book was planted when I was only nine years old, and my father gave me a gift that I'd never forget: a real, live, honest-to-goodness *horse.* She was a beautiful copper-colored palomino with a flowing golden mane. A wonderful dream had come true.

But a great deal of fear and trepidation soon followed. This small filly was huge in my eyes—I couldn't even see over her back, and with her frisky spirit, she was clearly more horse than I could handle.

To the farm hands and the would-be macho cowboys who hung around the large Midwestern farm where I kept my horse, my task was clear: *Take charge*. Show that horse who's boss.

This is easier said than done, especially when your opponent outweighs you by more than 900 pounds. If I could have taken charge, I would have. I wanted to show all those guys—and myself—that this horse would not, could not, defy and intimidate me.

But Copper was by nature lively and excitable and also spooked by the saddle and me on her back. Whenever she got nervous and jumpy, I got scared and shaky and frequently landed on the ground. Physically, I was never seriously injured when I was thrown in front of the onlooking men, but I was hurt emotionally, and my confidence and sense of control suffered. How was I ever going to get it right?

Nobody was forcing me to ride her. I could've chosen the more dependable, passive old quarter horse that was stabled with her. But even though I was scared, I was determined to learn to ride my frisky filly.

After I'd accumulated a number of bruised ribs and scraped knees, my father signed me up for riding lessons. He appreciated my determination to handle this horse, but didn't want me trampled to death in the process. My instructor was quick to teach me what every master rider knows how to do: to *SIT*...to *GET CENTERED* in the saddle.

It worked. Instead of keeping a tight grip on Copper's mane in a fearful attempt to hang on, I learned to let my legs become my balance and support, extending and reaching down, stabilizing my seat. I learned to rock with the motion of the horse, and my hands eased their death-grip on the reins, giving the horse some slack and more comfort.

Soon I sensed that, instead of my two legs, I had four solid ones that could carry me across the fields and down the winding paths. I could feel the rhythm of the horse beneath me—the rocking and the swell of muscles that moved her across the ground. Free from my awkward bouncing on her back, she began to relax her spine. Then I could persuade her to make turns with just a gentle touch to the side of her neck, rather than yanking on the reins and sawing at her tender mouth.

By mastering my own body and my own reactions to Copper's movements, I gradually learned to ride, and within a couple of years, all my fears had vanished as my fiery quarter horse and I became great partners instead of adversaries. Sometimes I'd ride bareback—no saddle, no bridle—just circling the open fields. I'd let Copper take the lead—letting her go wherever she wanted to go.

Other times I'd enter a contest, and I would TAKE CHARGE. Together we learned to flag race. In that sport, six barrels are set up over a fifty-yard span, and rider and horse are clocked within a hundredth of a second from starting line to finish. They must weave their way down the arena, snake between barrels without knocking any over, make a full 360 degree turn around the final barrel, and weave back to the finish line.

Back at the ranch, I'd be at it again. Consider the experience of being centered in the saddle and directing a 1,000 pound *Force*—furiously running the trails, weaving through the woods, plunging across streams, and scaling steep riverbanks. It felt as if it were I alone who possessed all this speed and strength—this agility and daring. Suddenly I was the athlete of my dreams. Transformed, I was no longer a scared, awkward little kid in a world of giants.

While I had neither the talent nor the will to carve out a great equestrian career, my early riding experiences left me with a deep interest in sports and the dynamics of peak athletic performance. Riding Copper taught me that it's possible to become so partnered with another being—so enmeshed both physically and psychically—that identities can merge into something greater: an expanded sense of self.

When you let go of your limited, individual identity and join with another in a shared purpose, the task at hand becomes in one sense easier, but in another, an even greater challenge. You are now required to motivate and control and direct a much larger, more energetic, and sometimes more fearful self. Faced with this larger task—this larger self, you can either give up, or you can triumph by increasing your capacity to TAKE CHARGE.

The capacity to take charge can be viewed as the development within oneself of a small but powerful "center of control"—a part of one's self that keeps the larger self from being lazy or fearful or unruly. Effective action is not happenstance. It is orchestrated from one's center.

In one of the more memorable scenes in the history of movie-making, Obi-Wan Kenobi, the great *Star Wars* guru of high performance and warriorship, blesses Luke Skywalker as he prepares for battle with the now famous words of encouragement: *MAY THE FORCE BE WITH YOU.*

Perhaps the concept that there's a Force that will serve on your behalf and help you to perform optimally as you seek to achieve your mission is more than you can handle. But there's another way to think about the Force. It is simply your own energy—your ten trillion or more individual cells that spark and fire and constitute who you are. It's your power—the stuff that humans are made of. You *are* self-existing, electrifying energy. You are a slice of the Force.

Our task is not so much to call upon this Force, hoping that it *will be* there for us. Rather, it is to recognize that the Force is already within us, always ready for us to draw upon. Our role is to appreciate and embrace it—not to be afraid of it—rather to be delighted in its presence, and to ride and guide it.

Some of us have less energy—less electricity—than others. Some of us are not well-suited for hundred-yard dashes or two-yard plunges up the middle into the end zone. Some of us are better suited for downhill skiing, where the forces of gravity provide much of the energy. The trick is to discover your playing field and do what you can do—with no grumbling about being too young or too old or too tall or too small.

Not everyone gets to experience the raising and harnessing of a real live horse. But each of us has a Force. Each of us has a store of energy—an electrical capacity. Everyone has a CHARGE.

Your first step in mastering your Self then is to:

TAKE CHARGE OF YOUR CHARGE

You have been given a Force to ride. Don't be frightened of this electrifying energy, trembling in its presence. Welcome it and be glad of it. Settle yourself at its center, guide and direct it, courageously, effectively. Joyfully get it to do what it's capable of doing—doing what it's eager to do.

Don't over-bridle it. Don't stifle it. But simultaneously don't let it grow unruly or out of control. Find the balance. Keep it frisky and vigorous, but stay in charge.

This chapter defined the larger Self and explored the concept of mastering one's energies. The next chapter introduces the Energy Cycle as a description of a successful act and as a specific strategy for attaining Self-mastery.

2

Get Your Act Together

Stroking a golf ball with accuracy, power, and fluidity is a successful act with a beginning, a middle, and an end. It is an Energy Cycle with a Preparation phase, an Execution phase, and a Completion phase. Master these three phases of the act and you will consistently perform at your best.

Above is the advice and diagram I give to people interested in improving their golf games. As a business consultant and performance coach, I find golf an excellent vehicle for teaching the management of one's energies and for the training and development of self-mastery. Below is an account of how coaching in this sport worked particularly well.

With a trim athletic build and muscular forearms, Jack had been quite a good golfer for much of his life—good enough to make the golf team at a Big Ten university, usually shooting in the low- to mid-seventies even on the most difficult courses. But by the ripe old age of thirty-five, Jack's game had fallen apart. He couldn't break out of the mid-eighties and was losing to players he knew he should've been able to beat. Frustration with his consistent under-performance led Jack to abandon competitive golf altogether.

Jack didn't need anyone to explain the root causes of his problems. He was acutely aware that he pressed himself too hard and wasn't resilient in the face of failure. He could be playing well, but as soon as he hit a couple of consecutive "bad shots," he'd tumble into his negative thinking and not manage to climb out.

In recent years Jack had become overly serious about everything. He described himself as a hard-working perfectionist who expected excellence from himself and everyone around him—at home, at the office, or wherever. Life had become not only frustrating, but exhausting.

Despite my own relative lack of skill at hitting a golf ball, I was confident that I could help Jack with the mental and emotional dynamics of playing the sport and that this in turn would not only help him with his golf score—it would help him become a better father, a better husband, and a better systems analyst and sales manger.

When a golfer stops trusting his swing and starts ruminating about past shots and fretting about future shots, no matter how talented he may be, he loses fluidity and doesn't perform at his potential.

Relaxation is a key component for optimal performance. "I felt relaxed out there today," athletes frequently remark when asked about their excellent performances. Of course, an athlete doesn't want to become overly relaxed. Performing at one's best requires a certain degree of emotional intensity.

After some discussion, Jack and I concurred that such intensity is a crucial ingredient for playing at one's best, and that it was too simple to say that his main objective should be to loosen up and learn to relax on the golf course. A delicate balance is what's called for, and we agreed that the most effective performance state can best be described by a combination of apparently contradictory terms. The ideal performance state is one of *Relaxed Intensity.*

Shortly after our first meeting, Jack and I met early on a July morning at the local golf range where we would begin our work in earnest. I reminded Jack that not being an accomplished golfer myself, I'd have absolutely nothing to say about how he gripped the club or the mechanics of his swing. Rather, I would assume that the technical aspects of his stroke were fundamentally sound.

After Jack stretched and took a few warm-up shots, I suggested that he imagine himself on an actual golf course. He should tee up and hit a series of shots, *acting as if* he were in a competitive situation and intent on doing his best.

My role was to observe. Shifting positions as if I had a camera and were shooting photographs from various angles, I noted every gesture and move—from the manner in which he approached the tee, to his furrowed brow and the tension visible in his jaw, hands, and gut.

As I watched Jack, the first thing that struck me was that he clamped his lower lip between his teeth as he swung at the ball. This biting gesture reflected Jack's mindset—angry and overly tense. Later I suggested to him that his aggressive stance and grimacing might have served him well as a middle linebacker for the Chicago Bears, but that this attitude wasn't appropriate for a round of golf.

What most drew my attention, though, was his breathing pattern before, during, and after his swinging of the club. Instead of taking a natural inhalation of air on his backswing, then swinging through the ball with a natural exhalation, Jack was *holding his breath* through the entire sequence. And he appeared never to take a good deep breath—neither before a shot nor between shots.

Despite the excess tension I observed, Jack was actually hitting long accurate drives. I was convinced, however, that greater fluidity could be added to his swing, and that when playing a four-and-a-half-hour round of competitive golf, he'd be better able to maintain his poise and composure if he made some basic changes.

I interrupted Jack's ball striking, and we stepped into the shade to discuss what I'd observed. I began by reminding Jack that the task of striking a ball with a club and getting that ball to its target constitutes a single *Energy Cycle.* A cycle consists of three phases—a *Beginning,* a *Middle,* and an *End*—more specifically, a *Preparation phase,* an *Execution phase,* and a *Completion phase.*

These phases are best performed with the right rhythm and flow if the entire act is carried out from beginning to end within a single, smooth, and well-integrated *breath cycle.*

So I advised Jack, "Think of the Energy Cycle as simply a *breath*. Pick up your club. Inhale on your *backswing*. Exhale on your *downswing,* then allow for the full *swing-through* as you finish off your stroke and pause to take note of what happened."

When he did as I recommended, Jack loved the results. Tension and frustration drained from his face. It wasn't as if he'd just scored a hole-in-one, or hit the longest drive of his life, but he experienced the exhilaration of it all. Immediately and instinctively, he understood that this was the right way to stroke a golf ball.

Jack had a "But of course!" reaction. Though trained in the Martial Arts, where breathing is coordinated with every movement, Jack somehow had never applied those lessons to golf. Now that I'd mentioned it and he'd tried it, the suggestion instantly and intuitively made all the sense in the world to Jack.

After Jack stroked about a dozen balls using this new breathing pattern, we added a new feature to his ritual. I instructed him to incorporate into his breathing pattern a distinct sound for each of the three phases of the cycle. After a cleansing exhalation, the breath cycle would unfold as follows:

> *Phase One*: As he commenced his backswing, allowing for a slow, natural inhalation of breath to be drawn in through his nose and pursed lips, the incoming air would make an anticipatory IIIIEEEE sound—like the sound of a black-belted Bruce Lee circling his opponent and gracefully readying himself for the big strike. It would be a time of high motivation with controlled intensity.

Phase Two: On the downswing, the exhalation of his breath would create an **O**OOOHHHH sound as Jack executed his shot with a swift, powerful striking of the ball.

Phase Three: Having completed the shot and turned fully toward the path of the ball and observing the results of his act, Jack transforms his breath into the sound of a soft sigh—an **A**AAAHHHH. It was a time to add the finishing touch and a short interval for rest and renewal.

As a way of helping Jack implant the sequential sounds of this three-phased structure in his mind, I suggested that he think: **I.O.A**. (pronounced *Iowa*).

I	II	III
Preparation Phase	*Execution Phase*	*Completion Phase*
Backswing	*Downswing*	*Swing-through*
I*IIIIEEEE*	***O****OOOHHHH*	***A****AHHHHHH*

Coordinating the sounds with the motions came easily to Jack, and for the next twenty minutes he evoked the disciplined and highly-focused meditative state of a martial artist as he performed the sacred ritual of teeing up one ball and then another—stroking long, powerful drives, punctuated by the sounds of the breath cycle:

I slowly and deliberately initiating his *backswing* on an inhalation...

II swiftly, powerfully executing his *downswing* on an exhalation...

III fully extending that exhalation with a completed *swing-through*.

After leaving the driving range we returned to my office and talked for a few hours about this new way of removing excess tension from his swing. I suggested that before stepping back into competitive play he should stroke a minimum of 3,000 golf balls in the spirit described above. For the next few months he was not to concern himself about specific results or his score. His attention instead would focus on the pleasant experience of simply stroking a ball within the three-phased structure of a relaxing breath cycle—ever mindful of the easy and rhythmic circular motion of swinging the club.

He would hone his ball striking skills in the manner of the black-belted martial artist who each day returns to the dojo and achieves grace in action through repetition and devotion to practice. With awareness that the starting point for any athletic move begins at the navel, Jack would center himself with a cleansing exhalation as he stood over the ball—inhale, make the turn, and then complete the circle with a full downswing and follow through.

Further to highlight the importance of breath, I noted that life begins with a first breath and ends with a last breath and that, in between, if we live long and vigorously, we get about 21,000 breath cycles per day—700 million in a lifetime. Jack's job was to stay totally attentive to a small portion of those breath cycles. For the next ninety days, he wasn't to think of time spent on the golf course as a time to play a competitive round of golf, but rather as a time to enjoy a round of seventy to eighty perfectly-executed breath cycles. It would only be incidental that within the structure of each breath cycle, he'd be stroking a little white ball.

It was fine that Jack liked to compete. It was fine that he enjoyed achieving a winning score. But I suggested that he'd do well to detach himself from the results of a particular shot and a particular round of golf. I encouraged him instead to focus on the process—on the Act itself. He was to experience fully that pure pleasure of just swinging the club—the sweet feel of connecting with the ball and the lovely sight of it sailing high and far.

Not thinking about competing while actually engaged in a fierce competition is, of course, easier said than done. But I had equipped Jack with an operating system for clearing his mind and maintaining his composure, his cool, during the heat of battle.

The next day, Jack went alone to the practice range to put the new program to another test. It worked well for him. Almost too well. He reported that he began hitting the ball with an ease that was so mesmerizing, it put him into an altered state of consciousness that felt "kind of spooky"—as if some form of black magic were at work. But then he got used to it and imagined he might well be feeling what the pros feel when they get into what they call "the zone"—or a "deep flow state."

As a systems analyst and computer programmer, Jack readily grasped the theory behind the technique. By getting him to focus his mind on the three phases of the Energy Cycle and on the sounds of his breathing pattern, we were blocking negative thoughts from entering his mind—in a sense, "jamming the system" and equipping him with a new "software program" that would calm his mind and guide his muscles.

Jack's adoption of the three-phased rhythm of *the act* helped move him into that state of doing in which he was neither overly excited nor complacent. When he commenced his backswing, his total attention was zeroed in precisely, leaving no room in his mind for distracting or self-defeating thoughts, second-guessing, or doubt. He merely breathed in, breathed out, and followed through, trusting that his performance would unfold smoothly and naturally, and that his club head would strike the ball with precision and power. By concentrating on the rhythm and the sounds of I-O-WA—representing the beginning, middle, and end of each act or Energy Cycle—Jack succeeded. His desired outcomes followed naturally from that process.

About three months after our meeting at the driving range, Jack phoned to tell me he'd just finished playing in a golf tournament sponsored by the large corporation he worked for. He not only won the long-ball contest, but the championship itself, turning in a score of seventy-five and taking home a tall, handsome trophy.

Eventually, Jack's progress reports got even cheerier as he incorporated the spirit of energy cycling into his everyday life. At home and at work, he enjoyed much better control of his emotions, referring to his new behavior as his "Zen-approach" to acting and re-acting with others. His new way of playing golf had become his Martial Art—his Yoga—his way of integrating body, mind, and spirit in whatever he was doing.

Jack had learned how to manage his energies.

Performing at your best begins with the discovery that a successful act is a well-managed Energy Cycle. The next three chapters will expand on the three phases of the cycle and provide a detailed description of the 12 powers of an optimal performer.

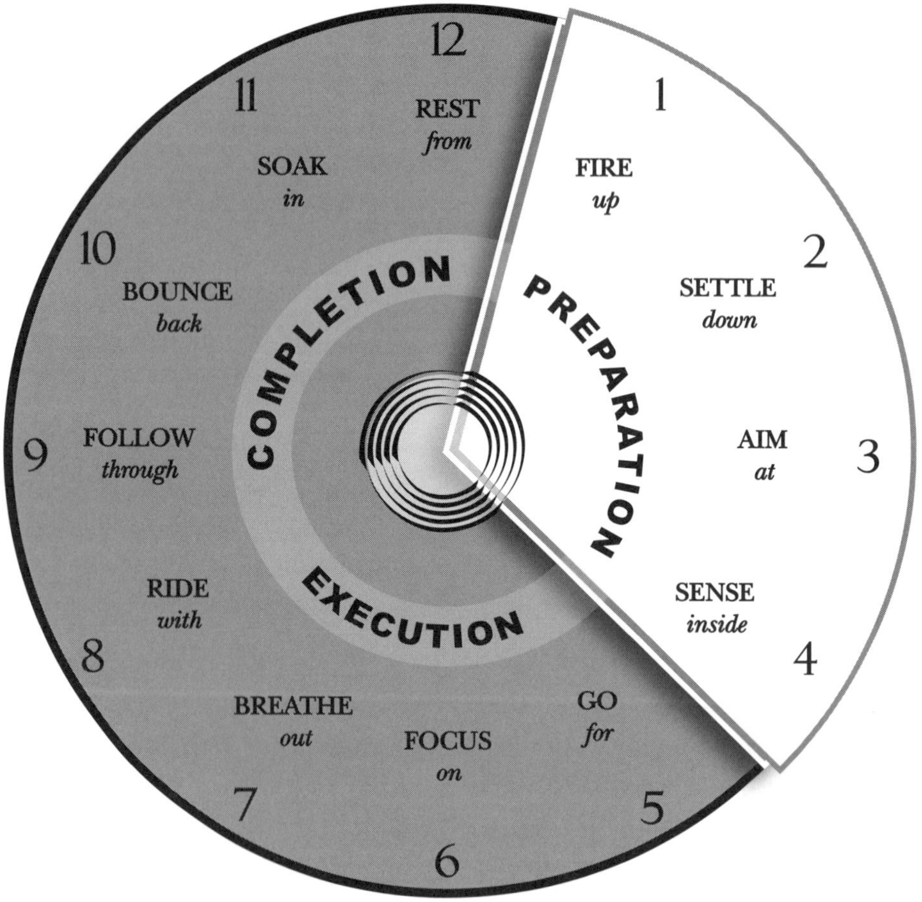

3

PREPARE

The Four Powers of Successful Preparation

Name of Power		Trigger Words
#1 Self-Motivation	....	Fire up
#2 Self-Control	....	Settle down
#3 Self- Direction	....	Aim at
#4 Self- Guidance	....	Sense inside

Mastery of an act—an Energy Cycle—depends on achieving mastery of Self. The first of three phases of the cycle is Preparation. Without successful preparation, no amount of natural ability or determination will enable your optimal performance. This chapter describes in vivid detail the four powers within the preparation phase—each a distinct capacity that provides the well-prepared performer with the *readiness to perform.* When you tell yourself to *Get ready* or *Get it together,* these are the powers you draw on.

The Preparation Phase of the Act can take place within milliseconds, and it's not always possible to distinguish each particular ability at work. A well-performed act will appear seamless, and distinct powers are usually not apparent. The steps are still there, but they are so smoothly integrated that they blend together. Rainbows do not really appear to us as a series of seven discrete color bands; the colors come together in a unified flow. The same is true of the preparation phase of the Energy Cycle.

In this chapter we deliberately single out the four powers and highlight them individually. Within the context of four separate sports, athletic acts are described in which the performer is called upon to make a sustained use of one particular power. Each power is illustrated with a vignette designed to capture its spirit and essence, and each power is accompanied by two short trigger words for easy reference and recall.

PREPARATION

Performance Power #1

Self-Motivation

> *"Success is not the result of spontaneous combustion. You must set yourself on fire."*
>
> —Reggie Leach, NHL hockey

Fire up:

~THE WORLD CLASS SPRINTER~

Three minutes to race time. Having trained for years, Olympic sprinters hover near the starting blocks in a controlled frenzy. The race of their lives will begin in minutes, and will last fewer than ten seconds. Absolute readiness is *everything.*

Yet the favorite feels sluggish today—the strain of the moment is draining him physically. He must summon excitement, pump adrenaline into his veins where weariness threatens to settle. In an instant, he must be at his most avid. He must be motivated, charged—or the moment will be forever lost.

He digs deep within. He inhales long and exhales hard— a full cleansing breath. Stirring the vast inner reserves that have brought him this far and fanning the flames of his passion for his sport, he seizes his opportunity:

This is it—the time and the place. This is the fun part—the running; the exciting part—the competition. This is all there is. There's nothing else.

Lifting his face skyward now, he's hot, radiating passion and energy for the task at hand. He absorbs the sun, the source of ALL energy, into his system, transforming it into the speed he'll need.

One minute. He pumps his legs, pounds his fists. He coaches himself, exhorting, imploring, demanding: *YES! YES! DO IT! GO!* All systems are positive, affirmative. Primed and ready.

And now this sprinter, this superb and finely-tuned athlete, is burning with desire. He moves into the blocks. Tingling with excitement, he crouches like a cat, ready to spring, to pounce. *Ten seconds.*

And now, a Chariot of Fire, a beaming ball of contained energy, he's ready to explode—to rise and fire on cue.

On the mark; fired-up; ready!

●●●●●●●●●●●●●

To succeed at any important enterprise, the first essential task is to ready yourself—to stimulate and motivate yourself sufficiently for the difficult journey ahead. We can all *fire up* occasionally, but the Maximum Performer must also be the Master Motivator, able to heat up for the fiercest battle, even when physical energy may be at its lowest ebb.

Ignite yourself into a burning intensity with your own Inner Coach. Cultivate that voice within you to spur yourself on to the performance of your lifetime in *your* arena of choice.

Develop: ***Power #1***

Remember: ***Self-Motivation***

Coach yourself to: ***Fire up***

PREPARATION

Performance Power #2

Self-Control

> *"...remain always cool and unruffled under all circumstances."*
> —Thomas Jefferson

Settle down:

~SWISH~

The rookie NBA point-guard with the league-leading 92% free-throw shooting average is somehow off the mark today. While all season long he's been automatic from the foul line—usually going the whole game without missing a single free throw, today all five of his attempts have clanked off the rim. It's perplexing. He ordinarily shoots foul shots with a blissful ease. His form is perfect. Once in practice, he made a bet that he could reel off 100 in a row—and he did it!

But we can guess what the problem is today. It's the first round of the playoffs and the biggest game of the rookie's life. He is overly excited, too intense. His "adrenaline high" enables him to race up and down the court and play excellent defense, but driving on that same nervous energy leaves him physically exhausted and throws his shot off.

Now with 1.5 seconds left on the clock and his team down by one point, the rookie is fouled again, and he's given two more chances at the line. It's simple. Just make these two shots and his team wins the game. It's a piece of cake—but he can feel his shoulders stiffening and his heart pounding, and he can't shake the image of his five botched attempts.

But then, as the ref hands him the ball, he senses what he needs to do. In his head he hears his high school coach: "Settle down. Take your time. Bring your energy down from your shoulders and your chest. Lower your heart rate. Get into your legs. Bend your knees. Feel your feet."

Ten seconds to do all that and then from this well-grounded position, the rookie goes into his regular routine: He exhales, bounces the ball twice, squares his feet to the basket, nestles the ball on his fingertips and, with a flick of the wrists, arches it toward the hoop.

SWISH! Game tied!

Again the same ritual—the same routine.

SWISH! Game over!

●●●●●●●●●●●●

In many tasks, the challenge may not be to fire up, but to settle down. Even if you never have the pressure of a game-winning opportunity on your fingertips, you're likely at some time to feel like the rookie free-throw shooter described above. You're highly motivated, but your adrenaline is pushing you too far—beyond what is helpful. Rein in that energy and settle it down. Calm those nerves, step up to the line, and perform at your best. Self-control is the second essential power in the preparation phase. Without it, all the internal fire you've ignited in the first stage will fizzle into a sub-optimal performance. With self-control, you're halfway to being thoroughly prepared.

Develop: ***Power #2***

Remember: ***Self-Control***

Train yourself to: ***Settle down***

PREPARATION

Performance Power #3

Self-Direction

> *"Have a purpose in life, and having it, throw into your work such strength of mind and muscle as God has given you."*
>
> —Thomas Carlyle, English writer

Aim At:

~ The Mark of a Champion ~

Each member of the Olympic archery team is a highly skilled athlete, but one stands above the rest. She is virtually certain to win the Gold Medal. If you ask her teammates why she wins almost every contest she enters, some will say it's because she's the best. Others, who study excellence more closely, will observe that she possesses some internal skill, some power that others lack or only partially master. Archery is a sport that comes down to one thing, they say: Aim. And not just the aim of a particular arrow, but aim in a larger sense.

Everything about this champion says: *"I know what I want and I aim to get it."* Everything about her reflects her dedication to a higher purpose—from the way she walks to how she talks and, in particular, to the precise and elegant way she picks up her bow, assumes her stance, and aligns herself perfectly with the target she is about to hit dead center.

Having aimed herself so precisely, the champion is truly ready when it comes time to aim her arrow. Her teammates—the potential silver and bronze medallists—are not as focused. They're well-prepared, certainly, but they lack the utter coherence of the champion. When she aims the arrow, every fiber in her body and every neuron in her brain are dedicated to and in harmony with her single resolve. Her goal is not merely to hit the bulls-eye; her goal is to make the universe wake up and take notice of an unrivaled excellence.

The champion's ability to set her mind, take aim, and direct herself toward the accomplishment of her objective is remarkable. She is crystal clear about what she wants and what she's capable of attaining.

●●●●●●●●●●●●●

Archery, like any endeavor, requires self-motivation and self-control, but it especially requires self-direction. You may not be inclined to take up a bow, but you can learn from the champion. Whether at play or at work, target your objectives. To prepare yourself successfully to execute whatever task you *are* inclined to take up, you must capture the spirit of the archer and learn to aim. Take time each day to develop your goals—clarify and condense them until you're sure what you want to aim at. Then, when you begin a task, the process of aiming your "arrow" will be fluid and uninterrupted.

Develop: ***Power #3***
Remember: ***Self-Direction***
Instruct yourself to: ***Aim At***

PREPARATION

Performance Power #4

Self-Guidance

> *"Happy are those who dream dreams*
> *and are ready to pay the price to make them come true."*
>
> —L.J Suenens, Writer and theologian

Sense Inside:

~Producing the Instant Pre-Play~

The lanky young golf pro with the swanky swing has a comfortable two-stroke lead with only one hole to go. Though he appears poised to achieve his first victory on the professional tour, this is when the young man has had a tendency to fold. More than a dozen times this year, he's been in a position to win, but in the final stretch, an errant shot or two robs him of a championship.

But this afternoon, the rookie is more confident, because he has a new trick—a technique he's developed since reading *Golf My Way,* written by his boyhood hero, Jack Nicklaus. Here's what Jack says about hitting winning golf shots:

> *I never hit a shot, not even in practice, without having a very sharp, in-focus picture of it in my head. It's like a color movie. First I "see" the ball where I want it to finish, nice and white and sitting up high on the bright green grass. Then the scene changes and I "see" the ball going there: its path, trajectory, and shape, even its fadeout, and the next scene shows me making the kind of swing that will turn the previous images into reality.*

For the past three days the rookie has been hitting drive after drive, long and straight—295 yards on average—into the middle of the fairway. On this last hole, he'll keep the negative thoughts—away. Indeed, he won't "think" at all. He'll *see* only positive images. He'll execute another of those long straight drives—assuring himself of victory.

The young man steps up to the eighteenth tee. He's fired up. He's settled down. He's taken aim. But before beginning his backswing, he pauses momentarily to guide himself into a trance-like state. Head down and eyes closed, he sees himself on the movie screen on the back of his eyelids launching another long drive that settles gently onto the middle of the freshly-cut fairway lawn. And within a few seconds he produces it—a 319 yard shot.

The rookie *guides* his imagination, evoking a clear full-color image of his next picture-perfect swing. He sees the little white ball sailing above the fairway, bouncing twenty yards from the green, and trickling to within two feet of the hole. The image is coupled with the wicked sound of the clubface smacking the small hard ball. In his heart and in his gut, he feels such deep satisfaction that he knows he'll replicate this wonderful shot that he senses within—not only "seeing" it, but also "hearing" it, and ultimately "feeling" it as well.

And having fully "sensed" the shot, he lets it happen. With grace and ease, he produces in reality that which moments ago existed only in his imagination.

•••••••••••••

When you get an internal sense of what you intend to do, you are providing yourself with an *instant pre-play* of the action. Few of us have the skill and the strength to wallop golf balls and expect them to sail consistently 300 yards down the middle of the fairway. But we all have the capacity to produce instant pre-plays of doable achievements.

It's easy: After you've fired up, settled down, and aimed at your target, get a clear, inner sense of how you are going to do it. Once this happens, your preparation is complete. You have drawn on your first four powers, and it's time to pass smoothly into the execution phase of your act. Are you ready?

Develop: ***Power #4***

Remember: ***Self-guidance***

Prompt yourself to: ***Sense Inside***

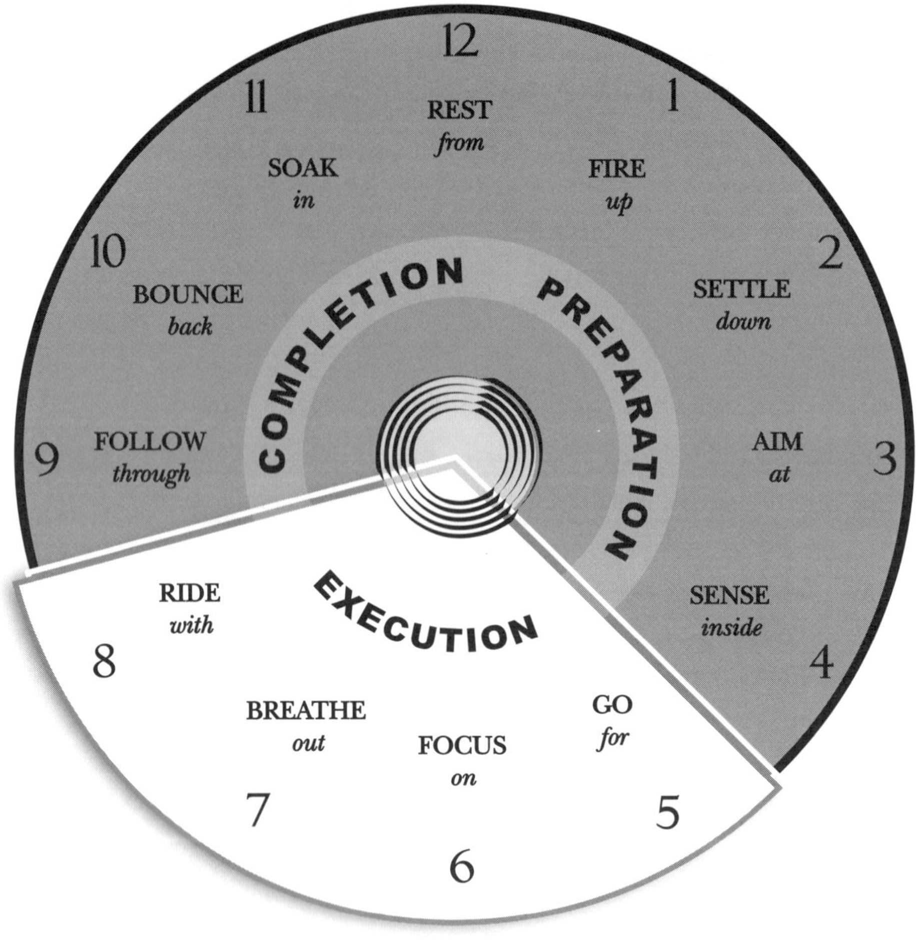
12
REST
from
1
FIRE
up
2
SETTLE
down
3
AIM
at
4
SENSE
inside
5
GO
for
6
FOCUS
on
7
BREATHE
out
8
RIDE
with
9
FOLLOW
through
10
BOUNCE
back
11
SOAK
in
PREPARATION
EXECUTION
COMPLETION

4

EXECUTE

THE FOUR POWERS OF EXCELLENT EXECUTION

Name of Power	Trigger Words
#5: Self-Encouragement	Go For
#6: Self-Discipline	Focus On
#7: Self-Expression	Breathe Out
#8: Self-Surrender	Ride With

Imagine you're asleep. Now you're awake. Did you observe the precise moment when you changed states? Probably not. The same is true of the segue between the *preparation* and *execution* phases of the Energy Cycle. The transition may take only milliseconds, but the difference is immense—much like moving from sleep to awareness.

While some people are good at getting themselves ready, they somehow falter in the middle of the act and ultimately fail to perform well.

It's one thing to climb the ladder and *prepare* for a triple flip off the high board. It's quite another to be courageous, take the leap, stay focused, and gracefully *execute* the feat. In this chapter we highlight the four powers that make it possible consistently and effectively to do what one has prepared to do.

EXECUTION

Performance Power #5

Self-Encouragement

> *"Be bold—*
> *and mighty forces will come to your aid."*
> —Basil King, Poet

Go for:

~TAKING THE PLUNGE~

A time-out has been called. Just one second left on the game clock with the home team down by four points. Sitting on the bench with his head buried in his hands is the burly 235-pound veteran fullback. He is nursing a sore ankle and a bruised ego and fretting about this next play, which will not only be the last of the game, but possibly also the last of his long and stellar career.

As one of the most feared and respected players in the National Football League, he has *crashed through, darted around, and leapt over* the bodies and outstretched arms of opposing linemen for thirteen years.

But for most of this afternoon, he has been stopped cold. Right now it doesn't matter even slightly that over the years he's rushed for a total of 18,983 yards. Suddenly, he's convinced that his entire career will be judged on this game alone, and by whether he can gain this next *one* yard—carrying the ball into the end-zone, gaining a victory, and moving his team on to the Superbowl.

For the first time in his career, the veteran is fearful. He wonders: *What if* all eleven defenders—more than a ton of muscle and sinew—anticipate his rush up the middle and simultaneously fling themselves at him, and he is smacked in mid-air and his neck is broken; *what if* his ankle gives out and he falls and he fumbles. *What if... What if... What if...*

Suddenly he sits straight up, digs deep within himself, and taps into his reservoir of courage. Within seconds, numerous scenes of heroic dashes through the line flash before his mind's eye. As quickly as he'd lost his backbone, he recovers it.

Let the defensive monsters snarl and growl. Let them try to protect their turf. He'll smash through any barrier they erect. The warrior summons his strength and energy. How? He growls at himself and pumps himself up. He envisions the End Zone as a sacred battleground he must enter and conquer. In short, he draws upon his well-developed capacity for *encouraging his self to go for* what he wants:

"This is my job...I am a warrior...I will charge forward...I will get there."

The fullback has the first four *powers*: He's FIRED for the task. He's SETTLED in his place. His AIM is certain. He SENSES the touchdown. Now his *act* will be energized by his number five power and he will GO FOR the end zone.

The play up the middle that everyone in the stadium expects is called. From a deep crouch, the high-powered fullback springs forward. Cradling the pigskin to his gut, he hurls himself headlong through the air, clambers over his opponents and—plunges unscathed into the Promised Land. Touchdown!

●●●●●●●●●●●●●

No matter how fired up you are, you can still be afraid. No matter how settled down you are, you can still have a touch of the butterflies. No matter how clearly aimed you are, you can still wonder what'll happen next. No matter how thoroughly you've played out the next move in your mind, outside thoughts may threaten your confidence. So now you have to go for it. Banish those fears, doubts, and stray thoughts. Encourage yourself at precisely the right moment: *I can do this!* You may not be hurtling headlong into a wall of behemoth linemen, but in your arena of choice, you can be the gutsy fullback who achieves his goal. What's the first step of execution? *Going for it.*

Develop: ***Power #5***

Remember: ***Self-Encouragement***

Urge yourself to: ***Go for***

EXECUTION

Performance Power #6

Self-Discipline

> *"The power of applying attention,*
> *steady and undissipated, to a single object,*
> *is the sure mark of a superior genius."*
>
> —Ralph Waldo Emerson

Focus On:

~2.5 Miles of Total Attention~

As the 3,000-meter Olympic bronze medallist nears the halfway point of her hometown five-mile community fun run, she knows she's not performing at her best today. The problem is obvious. She's not really committed to this race and her mind has been wandering from one distracting thought to the next.

Why did I let my friends talk me into this five-mile fun run?

I'm approaching 4,000 meters—this race is too long for me.

I should be back at school studying for my physiology exam.

But suddenly realizing her lack of focus, she resolves that from this spot in the road to the finish line she will excel. She gives herself a series of simple, straight-forward commands:

Snap out of it. Focus on your running. Pay attention.

Immediately things change. Like a horse with blinders, she narrows her attention on the road ahead. Extraneous thoughts no longer impinge. Suddenly it's all about running—only running. Running is all that she thinks about and all she questions:

Is it time to speed up and overtake the runners in front of me?

Do I have enough fuel in my tank?

Do I need a few sips of water?

How can I relieve that twitch in my left shoulder?

How's my breathing?

How fast do I need to run to win this thing?

Focus, focus, focus! Attention, attention, attention! These are her mantras. Her mind may want to wander off the path like a drunken donkey, but she keeps bringing herself back to the white line running down the center of the road.

For the next 2.5 miles, she will remain wholeheartedly involved in putting one foot in front of the other. Her mind will stay focused on running—simply running. Just doing what she's doing at the time she's doing it. Discipline, discipline, discipline! With 3,000 meters (1.86 miles) to go, she tells herself that this is her race now—just a short sprint home.

And indeed it is! As expected, the Olympian champ excels—she's the first to cross the finish line.

●●●●●●●●●●●●●

Once you've decided to *go for* a goal, you're clearly into the heart of executing the performance required to reach it. But in order to execute fully, you must maintain your *focus on* that goal, whether it's getting a degree or landing that job you have always wanted. The ability to focus complete attention on the task at hand is a matter of self-discipline. To become a maximum performer in the arena of your choice, it's not necessary to enter five-mile races, but it can be very useful to capture the spirit of the 3,000-meter runner. Think of yourself as a dedicated "Olympian"—a performer able to stick to a path, pay attention, and make that final sprint home.

Develop: ***Power #6***

Remember: ***Self-Discipline***

Force yourself to: ***Focus on***

EXECUTION

Performance Power #7

Self-Expression

> *"Fear is just excitement without breath."*
>
> —Fritz Pearls, Psychoanalyst

Breathe out:

~The Dance of Tennis~

When the long-legged beauty with the olive skin and expressive eyes was asked why she had given up a promising stage and dance career to pursue her dream of becoming a professional tennis player, her answer was short and concise:

"It's still all about dance. And tennis provides me with a bigger stage."

And now her dream had come true:

Wimbledon—center court—championship match!

She's playing well, but she's down 3-1 in the final set. The young star has somehow retreated into an overly-cautious style of play and instead of moving with her customary exuberance and grace, her steps appear heavy. Instead of her usual grin and easy manner, she's scowling, slumping her shoulders, dropping her head. As if afraid of making a mistake, she appears to be deliberately holding herself back—*de*pressing instead of *ex*pressing her naturally effervescent *self.* But in the few moments of reflection before the start of the fifth game, she reminds herself of her own axioms for success:

Make it fun. Be a performer. Dance. Be expressive. Have no fear. Breathe out.

And now, as suddenly as she'd allowed herself to collapse inward and restrain her moves, she once again starts giving her all—holding nothing back.

Again her swing is free. Her sweeping backhands and slashing forehands are punctuated with vigorous, audible exhalations. The ball, infused with topspin, darts low and swift over the net into her opponent's court.

No longer tight-lipped and constrained, she resumes the role of dominant performing artist, taking over the stage and giving full expression to her athleticism and artistic gifts.

The star is dancing.

●●●●●●●●●●●●●

There is a saying in yoga: "Proper breathing is the answer to everything." Breathing is key to allowing yourself to express—to execute—all that you're capable of. From the tennis star who dances on the grass at Wimbledon to the backyard hoops-shooter to the top roller at the weekly bowling league, knowing when to *breathe out* helps ensure an optimal performance. Breathing out, expressing yourself, is your pivotal power: you've prepared, you've begun and focused on your task, and now you're beginning to wrap up your execution, readying yourself to enter the completion phase. Always, *always* remember to breathe out!

Develop: ***Power #7***

Remember: ***Self-Expression***

Press yourself to: ***Breathe out***

EXECUTION

Performance Power #8

Self-Surrender

> *"Lean forward and have faith."*
>
> —John Bradley Carroll, Psychologist

Ride with:

~GOING WITH THE FLOW~

The Olympic ski team candidate isn't doing well on the icy slopes of this steep, unfamiliar mountain. Gusts of wind and rapidly shifting snow conditions keep throwing her off her edges. The harder she tries to carve her turns and maintain her downhill speed, the worse it gets.

She *hates* this mountain. It's a monster. It's her enemy, and it's crushing her. But she resolves that tomorrow will be different. By sheer force of will, she'll beat this mountain into submission. She will conquer it.

After reviewing the videotapes of her practice runs, and following a good night's sleep, complete with pleasant dreams, she awakens in a new frame of mind with an entirely new strategy.

She doesn't need to force her will on this mountain and attempt to *conquer* it. She needs to *surrender* herself to it and be its *friend.*

Let the wind howl. Let the snow conditions change. Let the vertical drop and the forces of gravity exert their relentless pull. She won't fight this monster—she'll join forces with it—center herself on its back and *ride with* it to the finish line.

And so she does. Without over-controlling and over-exerting herself, she's no longer afraid of falling and failing. By yielding to and merging with the mountain, she builds her speed and carves her turns with grace and ease.

The young skier is no longer trapped in a struggle. She's at one with her skis, with the mountain—at one with the world—and on her way to the Gold.

Flying down a mountain at breakneck speed—trusting in a pair of skis and the forces of nature—isn't for everyone. But whatever the context, there comes a time when it's more important to yield and to merge with existing energies than to insist on further asserting one's self. A perfect act involves self-surrender. It requires a moment or more of just letting things happen. It requires not merely *doing*, but also *allowing* a thing to be done.

All that remains is the completion phase of your act.

Develop: ***Power #8***

Remember: ***Self-Surrender***

Let yourself: ***Ride with***

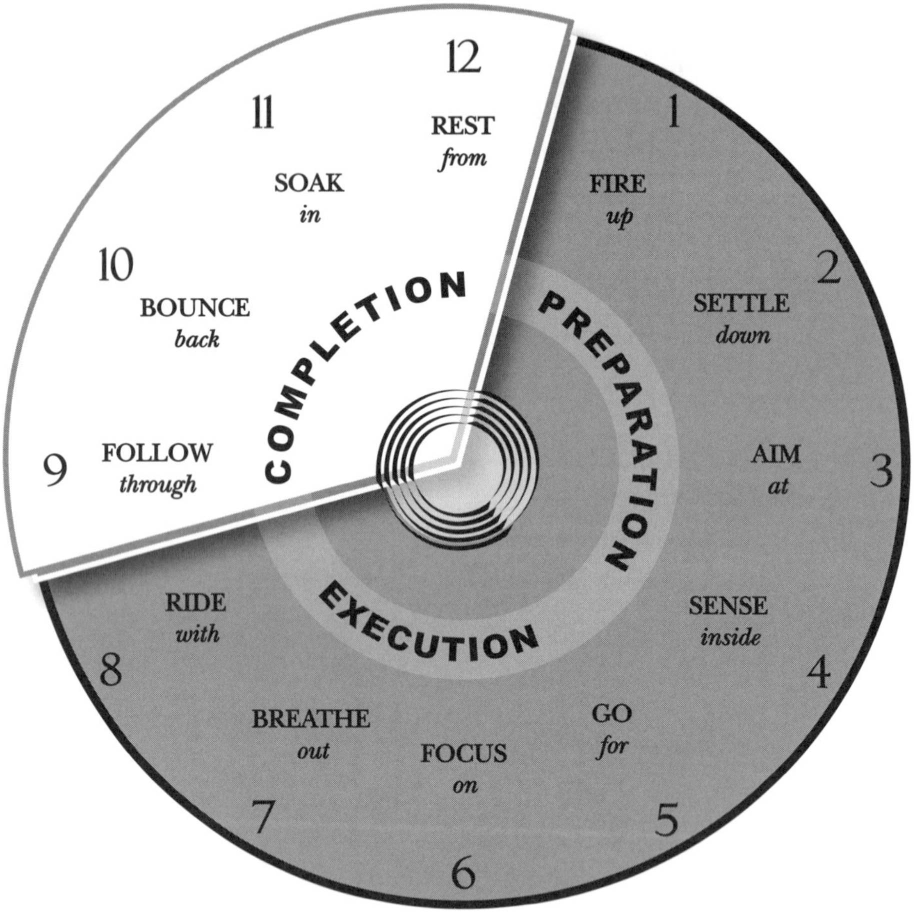
12
REST
from
11
SOAK
in
10
BOUNCE
back
9
FOLLOW
through
COMPLETION
1
FIRE
up
2
SETTLE
down
3
AIM
at
4
SENSE
inside
PREPARATION
5
GO
for
6
FOCUS
on
7
BREATHE
out
8
RIDE
with
EXECUTION

5

COMPLETE

THE FOUR POWERS OF FULL COMPLETION

Name of Power	Trigger Words
#9 Self-Fulfillment	Follow Through
#10 Self-Trust	Bounce Back
#11Self-Reflection	Soak In
#12 Self-Regeneration	Rest From

The ground is prepared. The seed is planted. Now it's harvest time.

The performer reaps her reward in the Completion Phase of the Energy Cycle.

Whether it is the Olympic diver going for the gold or the professional golfer going for the green, a mark of the champion performer is the full and flourishing follow-through that brings the act to a glorious completion.

In addition to this finishing touch, mastery of the Completion Phase is characterized by resilience and perspective—by the performer's capacity to reflect and make adjustments.

This phase of the act is also marked by the performer's ability to revitalize her energies and recapture her enthusiasm for the successful completion of the acts to follow.

This chapter highlights the four powers of the highly productive performer.

COMPLETION

Performance Power #9

Self-Fulfillment

> *"The greatest discovery of my generation is that human beings can alter their lives by altering their attitudes of mind."*
>
> —William James, American psychologist and philosopher

Follow through:

~THE FINAL TOUCH~

With fifty years of bowling experience under his belt and nearly as much analysis of his game in his head, the stocky gray-haired mechanical engineer is on the verge of rolling his first perfect 300 game. One more strike, and he will have fulfilled a life-long dream.

Small wonder this amateur bowler is so confident and composed. It would be only natural for him to be remembering the six previous times in his life when he'd rolled eleven, yet failed to roll a twelfth perfect ball. Each time he had failed to fulfill his dream.

But no longer conflicted about excellence, this man has a new attitude. His unconscious mind is not about to sabotage his score because an amateur doesn't deserve to roll a perfect game, or because the attention would embarrass him. He's ready, at last, to fulfill his lifelong quest.

His attitude is simply this:

I want this next strike. I deserve it. I'm going to get it.

And as he steps to the line, he murmurs:

"Follow Through—Fulfill Thyself."

He faces the pins, steps forward, and delivers the ball on a smooth exhalation. His hand and arm follow this natural arc to shoulder height and upward—full extension. There's no holding back—no hesitation at the moment of release. There's no doubt in this man's mind about what he wants to accomplish.

He adds his finishing touch, guiding the ball down the alley and rotating it into a well-timed hook toward the "pocket."

Wham! A strike! Twelfth in a row!

A perfect game! Fulfillment!

●●●●●●●●●●●●●

Whatever your arena, always follow through on what you've set out to accomplish. Whether it's your twelfth strike sailing down the lane, your finger roll after releasing a free throw, your picture-perfect pose after hitting a 200-yard three-iron over water to the green, or your last hundred footfalls in a long-distance race, following through with confidence and enthusiasm is essential. The *riding with* you did at the end of the performance phase brought you close to your goal. Now you need to summon and sustain one last burst of energy to successfully complete your act. What you've set out to achieve is within your grasp—you can taste it, as they say, so don't let it elude you now! Apply the finishing touches to attain what you've envisioned.

Complete your acts—not with a withholding whimper, but with a grand, final, full-throttle flourish. *Follow through!*

Develop: ***Power #9***

Remember: ***Self-Fulfillment***

Allow yourself to: ***Follow through***

COMPLETION

Performance Power #10

Self-Trust

> *"Just trust yourself,*
> *then you will know how to live."*
>
> —Johann Wolfgang von Goethe,
> German writer and poet

Bounce back:

~Up From the Depths~

Sitting hunched with a big white towel draped over her head, the Olympic diving champion is uncharacteristically teary-eyed and morose. Not a good day. Her scores were a disaster, and on the last of her dives, she sprang high, tucked in too close to the board, and severely scraped and bruised her shins and ankles.

But this champion is known for her capacity to bounce back from the depths. By nightfall she's forgotten her misfortunes. Trusting that she'll rise again to meet the challenges of a new day, she sleeps soundly and dreams glorious dreams of soaring through the air and winning the gold. In the morning she awakens rested and refreshed.

It's not surprising that this high diver has the ability to spring back from adversity. Rebounding is an inherent requirement of the sport. You fly off a high board, do triple flips in the air, and knife with great speed into the water—fingertips hitting the cement floor of the pool. But flexible, and resilient, and buoyant, you bounce back. You shoot to the surface, climb the ladder, and ready yourself for your next dive.

Diving is about rebounding and recovering and trusting. It is about knowing that, after you take the plunge, you'll return from the depths. You'll spring from the darkness. As expected, our champion does exactly that. She recovers. Five beautiful dives, all with a high degree of difficulty, bring her to the top of the leader board. She carries the day. She's on her way to the gold.

●●●●●●●●●●●●

Whether we think of ourselves as resilient or not, we have all, at one time or another, *bounced back*. We all go through adversity and discover a source of power that enables us to carry on. This power is your tenth in the Energy Cycle—your capacity for recovery. Even if you can't perform triple flips off the high board, you can emulate the high diver by taking the plunge, sinking to the depths, and trusting that you'll rise again, ready and eager for your next act.

Develop: ***Power #10***

Remember: ***Self-trust***

Expect yourself to: ***Bounce Back***

COMPLETION

Performance Power #11

Self-Reflection

> *"Any activity becomes creative when the doer cares about doing it right, or better."*
>
> —John Updike, American writer and poet

Soak in:

~TAKING NOTE~

It is the halfway mark of the season and the stocky red-haired third baseman with the .329 lifetime batting average is in a slump. Convinced that something is wrong with the way he's swinging the bat, he engages in an exercise that has always worked well for him: a *video-analysis session.*

Sitting in his large leather recliner chair with soft music playing in the background, the veteran slugger picks up his remote control and reviews slow-motion replays of his last twenty-four times at bat. A painful exercise, but it's time for him to acknowledge and reflect upon what he has been doing, and what he hasn't been doing. It's feedback time.

Like a master painter viewing a work of art, he notices dozens of little shadings and nuances that the uninitiated eye would never discern. And while he notes what he doesn't like, he connects nearly simultaneously with the images of his mistakes as they appear on the screen, seeing what he could have and should have done, rather than merely what he had been doing.

He lowers himself more comfortably into his chair, as a new set of images appear on the screen—slow motion replays of his all-time favorite times at bat. He soaks them all in. He observes his every movement—his entrance into the batting box, the shuffling of his feet, his grip on the bat, the turn of the hips, his long fluid follow through.

The videotape serves as more than a reminder of what he has accomplished. It also tells him how he did it, revealing effective swing mechanics, reawakening muscle memories, evoking the exhilaration of successful at-bats as the batter bathes in his new spirit of confidence.

It's a big step from a leather recliner chair and a field of dreams to the gritty dust of a real batter's box in a major league park. But the veteran has rediscovered the tempo and rhythm of his swing, and in the very next game, he breaks out of his slump.

Three times at bat.

Wham! Wham! Wham!

Three crisp line drives over the shortstop's head and into left field.

●●●●●●●●●●●●

Children learn possibly the most important words they'll ever hear before they are allowed to cross the street: "Stop, look, and listen."

Most of us internalize this ritual and forget the phrase. It's useful, however, to remember those words during the latter stages of a successful performance. You must *soak it all in* by attending to your act, by reflecting on your performance, and by comparing it to your goals—just like the batter with his video replays.

How are you doing? What's going right? What's going wrong?

Bask in your accomplishments. Don't hide from your mistakes. Reflect and discover.

Be a *constructive* critic of your own performance—knowing that how and what you say to yourself as you complete your present act will have an impact on your next act—your next Energy Cycle.

Develop: ***Performance Power #11***

Remember: ***Self-Reflection***

Teach yourself to: ***Soak in***

COMPLETION

Performance Power #12

Self-Regeneration

> *"All work and no rest takes the spring and bound out of the most vigorous life. Time spent in judicious resting is not wasted, but time gained."*
>
> —J.B. Grier, American writer

Rest from:

~ Time to Stop~

A beautiful snow-capped peak has been silhouetted to his left against a clear blue sky most of the day, but within the last hours, a few black clouds make more urgent the mountaineer's labors up the sheer rock wall. With one final valiant effort of mind and muscle, he hoists himself up and over a foreboding overhang, plopping his outstretched body onto a welcoming ridge, jutting just beyond the halfway point of this treacherous climb.

After catching his breath and resting his limbs briefly, he feels the press of time. He rises, hoping to push himself onward and upward another 1,000 meters to the top of the cliff.

But no sooner does he start to move than he hears the urgings of a very different voice, advising him from within:

"Stay where you are. Wait out the storm. Take rest from your journey."

And he does. Using hardware, harness, and lengths of rope, the mountaineer secures himself against a fall into the abyss. He settles in for the night.

Lying on his back, arms crossed, he breathes rhythmically, relaxing himself so deeply and completely that he sleeps through the storm and awakens in the morning as well-rested as if he'd spent the night at home in his own comfortable bed.

This ability to bivouac—to stop and rest on a tiny ledge near the top of a towering monolith, is in many ways the most remarkable aspect of this man's climbing power.

As dawn breaks, the regenerated mountaineer greets a beautiful new day and eagerly resumes his climb.

By mid-morning he's rejoicing on top of the mountain.

●●●●●●●●●●●●●

Even after years of training, most of us would still be ill-equipped to sleep through the middle of a storm on a small rock ledge near the top of a towering cliff. But if you care to fulfill your dreams and to scale the heights in your chosen arena, you must follow the lead of the expert climber. The secret to peak performance and the achievement of goals lies in the management of one's energies—making certain that periods of intense activity are followed by regular periods of rest and recovery. You must be ready not just to push on to the pinnacle, but also to pause when your body, mind, and instincts tell you it is time to do so.

The optimal performer knows how, when, where, and why to stop and recoup his energies—to rest.

Develop: ***Power #12***

Remember: ***Self-Regeneration***

Permit yourself to: ***Rest from***

In this chapter and over the course of the two previous chapters, we've described twelve distinct sports situations. In each situation, we singled out and highlighted the performer's use of one particular power. Our intent was to capture the spirit and essence of each of the individual powers. Once a performer develops and integrates the powers of the energy cycle, the deliberate and conscious accessing of those powers become less and less necessary. In the next chapter we turn again to the sport of baseball. But this time we illustrate how, in the process of carrying out the single act of hitting a baseball, the performer demonstrates his use of the 13th Power, namely the integration of all 12 powers.

6

Step Up to the Plate

On a bright day in July, when the blue of the sky is palpable, and the air just hot enough that an occasional breeze feels like a divine breath, a baseball game unfolds. Thousands of fans, most wearing their team's white and blue, fill the stadium. In the early innings they'd milled about, wolfed down hot dogs, or consulted their programs and kept track of the game's statistics. But now it's the ninth inning and the home team trails by a single run. Yearning to bring the action close, everyone leans forward.

But there's one player they can't see no matter how they crane their necks or shift in their seats. Deep in the shadows of the dugout sits the aged hero Luke.

Luke lounges on the bench among the growing piles of sunflower seeds and other debris. Although he hasn't played at all, he's tired. He feels his forty-two years today. His right leg is permanently crooked after three knee operations, he stoops a little due to a chronically sore back, and his hair is gray and thinning. When he takes off his cap, he realizes he may resemble an aging investment banker more than a major league baseball player.

People ask Luke why he sticks with the game, and he tells them it's because he's an old warrior. He may have already seen the worst of battles, but he feels he can still *perform*.

Now, with two outs in this last inning, the manager calls for Luke. With a grunt and a nod, the old warrior rises from the bench and clutches his bat. The crowd erupts into cheers when his name is announced. His fans' exuberance diminishes but cannot entirely erase his pain. Big Luke grimaces as he steps toward the plate.

Hitting a baseball is frequently described as one of the most difficult of all athletic acts—an act requiring precise movement, timing, and eye-hand coordination. Luke must expertly garner all twelve performance powers if he's to hit the next 97-mph pitch fired his way. (See Figure 6.1)

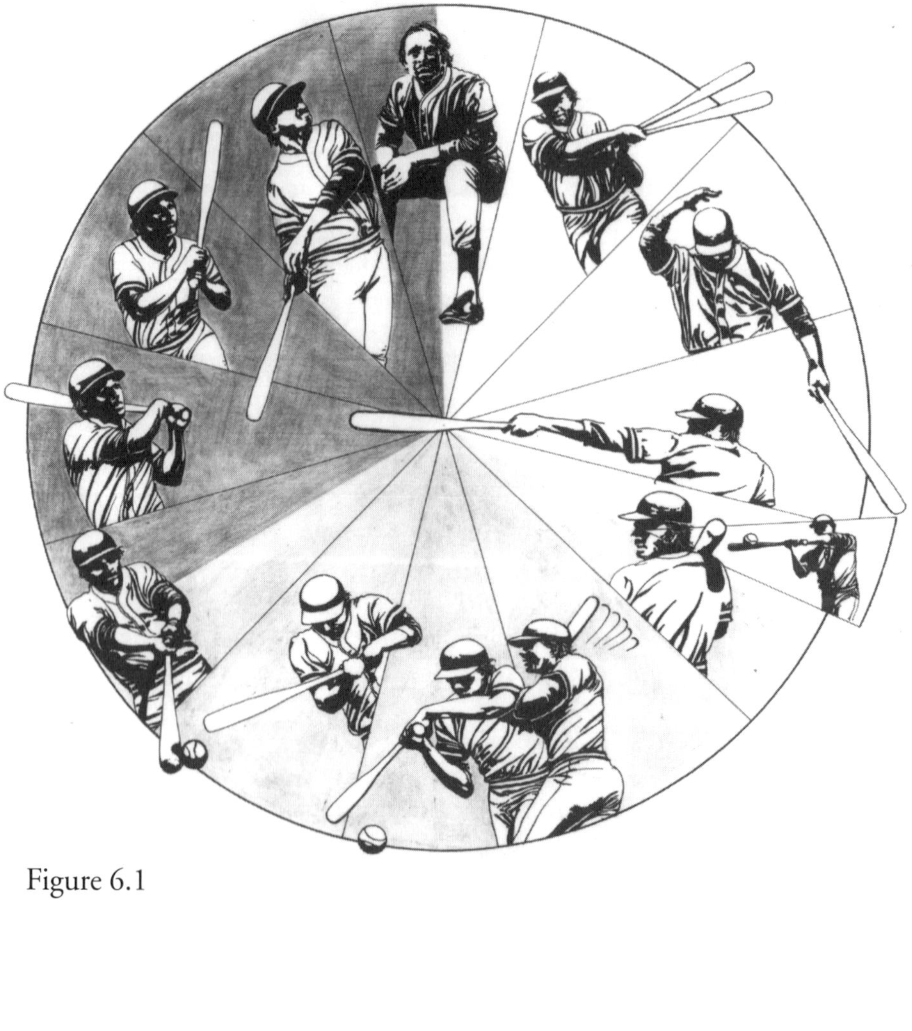

Figure 6.1

PREPARATION

Before entering the batter's box Luke initiates a few-second ritual. It marks the beginning of his *act*. He taps his left foot twice with the bat, his right foot once, adjusts his helmet, rubs his left shoulder, and murmurs to himself: "*Time to fight.*" Lethargy drains from his body as he summons the adrenaline to confront the challenge at hand. His body screams at him to explode into motion. Luke FIRES UP.

But the clenching of Luke's stomach and the unfocused energy in his limbs mean he's more eager than ready. Luke takes three seconds to ground himself. He touches the plate with his bat and digs his cleats into the dirt while returning the pitcher's unwavering stare. He steadies himself for the pitch. Luke SETTLES DOWN.

Now Luke targets his objectives:

Make solid contact. Take a full swing. Win the game.

He takes AIM AT the bleachers.

The pitcher completes his wind-up and moves toward the plate. Just before the ball leaves the hurler's hand, Luke summons a mental picture of his goal already accomplished: He hears the roar of the crowd and the smack of the bat at the moment of contact; it sounds like the shattering of bones. He sees the ball pop off the wood of the bat and begin its trajectory—high and far through the clear blue sky. Luke has a distinct INSIDE SENSE of what he intends to do.

By FIRING UP, SETTLING DOWN, AIMING AT, and SENSING INSIDE, Luke has PREPARED himself for the pitch. He has centered his desire and energy on the well-imagined outcome.

Now he's ready to attack. He's ready for the execution phase of the act.

EXECUTION

The swing takes place within milliseconds. But unconsciously and instantaneously the batter activates all four powers of the execution phase of the cycle. The pitch is hurled his way at 97 mph, but so composed and attentive is Luke that the small white leather covered ball, just 9 inches in circumference, with 108 stitches of waxed red cotton thread, appears as big as a grapefruit and seems to move toward him in slow motion.

Luke knows this one is his. He encourages himself to GO FOR it. His right heel lifts as he begins his lean into the pitch. He avoids distractions as his eyes zero in like lasers on the path of the ball. He stays FOCUSED ON the task at hand.

Luke releases the energy he has prepared for this precise moment as he whips his bat into the pitch. A full expression of air rushes from his lungs. He smacks the ball cleanly in an immense exhalation of energy. An explosion of wood meets hide as Luke BREATHES OUT.

The bat, now three-quarters of the way across his body, has a momentum exceeding Luke's own strength—surpassing his own will. The ball has leapt off his bat, yet Luke still RIDES WITH the swing. He merges with the motion of the bat and surrenders himself to the direction of its force.

The first four steps of the act allowed Luke to prepare for the pitch. The subsequent four steps allowed him to execute.

GOING FOR his goal started him on his path.

FOCUSING ON the pitch kept him on his path.

BREATHING OUT punctuated his energy.

RIDING WITH his own momentum maintained the flow of his swing.

COMPLETION

The bat whips across Luke's body, now fully extended, and he allows his explosive swing to FOLLOW THROUGH to completion.

Luke realizes that this stage of the swing is as crucial as any other. The bat must not be restrained. Its path will end only when the bat finally thuds to a halt against his coiled back muscles. As rapidly as he extended himself, with a full follow through of his arms and twisting and coiling of his legs and hips, Luke now quickly *uncoils*. Trusting in the resiliency of mind and muscle, he BOUNCES BACK from exhaustive action and regains his centered stance.

As Luke drops his bat and begins his run toward first base, the ball completes its arc high above the outfielder's outstretched glove. The hush of the crowd gives way to a rush of chaos. Fans scramble for the ball, still bouncing around in the bleachers. Luke's teammates stream from the dugout in exaltation.

Yet even in the din of celebration, Luke is serene. He SOAKS IN the experience of hitting the game-winning homer.

Luke reflects on the results, savors the moment. He quietly acknowledges that these opportunities—these moments of frenzied jubilation—are growing less frequent.

Rounding the bases is a formality. Before that first step he pauses…and does *nothing*. It's a minor moment of regeneration—a REST FROM performance and a brief foreshadowing of a much larger rest to come.

Much as Luke relishes his trot around the bases and the adulation of the crowd, he knows that baseball is a game of cycles: four bases in the shape of a diamond, three outs to an inning, nine innings to a game.

Baseball won't stop for this moment.

And Luke will perform again.

●●●●●●●●●●●●●

In this chapter, Luke demonstrated Self-mastery—his 13th Power—by gathering and integrating all 12 Powers of the Energy Cycle within the process of a single warrior-like act. In the next chapter, a very different performer in a very different arena will demonstrate the magic of the 13th Power.

7

Let Yourself Soar

The crowd's excitement echoes loudly off the steamy tile walls and the rippling surface of the indoor pool. But as the next diver climbs to the top of the diving board, the crowd quiets, watching her.

She is Nerissa—grace in action. Her shoulders and thighs have the smooth, powerful muscularity of the practiced diver. Her head is erect as she stares straight ahead. There are qualities about her that set her apart from the other young female divers. She's passionate, intense, and yet she's relaxed, revealing an innate poise that infuses her every move.

Nerissa positions herself carefully at the edge of the diving board for a back layout dive. A hush settles over the arena. Nerissa, like any diver, needs these moments of silence. The pause creates more than a dramatic effect. To the casual observer, nothing happens in that moment, but inwardly, Nerissa is at work. In her mind's eye she forms a vivid picture of what she intends to do. She remembers, dreams, and gets the feel of what she wants to express.

Another second's pause, then she lifts off and soars through the air and over the water, her body extending into a beautiful arc. Her dive is a work of art painted on an airy surface. No brush, no canvas, she uses her Self. Nerissa is the paint, the painter, and the painted. Her dive appears effortless, as though an unseen force were propelling her through the air and water. Her dive completed, she surfaces, reborn, to the applause of the spectators.

When Nerissa climbs out of the pool and resumes her place on the bench, she sits serenely, utterly at rest. She is able to isolate herself from the clamor around her, finding the peaceful, still center within herself. Yet she's neither idle nor passive. Far from it. Purposefully restful, she soaks in the electricity flooding the arena. Calmly, she awaits her next dive.

In the previous chapter we described the 12 Powers of the heroic Luke, as he stepped up to the plate and used his warrior mentality, his rippling muscles, and his mighty bat to belt out a home run. In this chapter we turn to the sport of high diving and examine the dynamics of a very different act—an act that reveals not only great *athleticism*, but superb *artistry*, as well.

When a batter hits a home run, he does not put extra points on the scoreboard if he does it beautifully. All that matters is that he smacks the ball over the fence. But in diving, a high score is attained not only by technically executing all the proper twists and turns, but by also performing the dive gracefully—artfully—beautifully.

With the experience of our imagined ultimate performer Nerissa, we illustrate that, while her act differs greatly from slamming a baseball, those same twelve fundamental powers are very much in evidence as she strives to create a perfect dive and earn an Olympic gold medal.

A superb athlete reveals the heart of the achievement process in a single act. When a master tennis player executes an adept serve, or a figure skater glides elegantly across the ice and manages a perfect triple axel, or a fine diver such as Nerissa parts the waters with the graceful entry of her body, the audience is seeing only a single cycle of an overall excellent performance. But that individual cycle is actually the sum total of a series of small distinct moves made possible by a set of powers that have been developed and internalized over a period of years. What the audience enjoys seeing is the athlete's success in blending these distinct moves into a series of seamless, unified acts.

The twelve individual powers of the optimal performer can be seen as resembling the "isolations" that a ballet dancer practices at the barre. A dancer masters them all so that the final product, her performance, appears fluid and seamless. But to get a deeper understanding of how the performer is able to accomplish what she does, it is helpful to isolate and distinguish the three phases and 12 Powers of the act. (See Figure 7.1)

Figure 7.1

PREPARATION

After a period of rest, waiting on the bench for her next dive, Nerissa begins to FIRE UP, summoning a surge in energy, an intense desire to do well. She doesn't shrink from this powerful force or let it unnerve her. She welcomes the wave of energy. Further, she enhances this energy by taking practical steps: by exercising, doing her warm-up routine, getting her blood flowing. She *motivates* herself.

But desire and fire are not sufficient. Nerissa must contain that energy. She must SETTLE DOWN. As she calmly walks to the edge of the diving board, all her excess energy is "grounded." Nerissa is in *control* of the moment—in *control* of the space—in *control* of her *self.* Still full of energy, she's able to harness it. She attains that precise balance of tension and relaxation that she needs to perform well.

Now Nerissa raises her arms until they point straight ahead. She appears to AIM AT something, suggesting that she has a definite goal in mind and that she intends to achieve it. Her stance radiates purpose and *self-direction.*

Nerissa's arms drop to her side. She holds still. It's the final stage of the preparation phase—the dramatic pause. This is what I call the "instant preplay." Nerissa takes the time to SENSE INSIDE the entire act. She travels inward for a moment and *guides herself* into a visualization of a perfect dive—the successful completion of the act. She visualizes it so precisely and feels it so deeply that it begins to happen. She starts to lift off.

The preparation phase is over.

EXECUTION

Nerissa now demonstrates her ability to GO FOR her dreams. She doesn't hold back; she *encourages* herself to take the risk. Some people get stuck in their dreams, never leaving the diving board or faltering on take-off, only to flop awkwardly into the water. Not Nerissa.

She allows herself to FOCUS ON her dream. She doesn't permit external events—the noise of the crowd, the restless movements of the spectators, or internal matters—her own anxieties and insecurities, to distract her. She exercises *self-discipline* and stays on target.

Her next move demonstrates another important principle. As sportswriters say, people often "choke" or lose their nerve when called upon to perform. In reality, this is more than just a figure of speech. At such times, anxious performers literally hold their breath, or they inhale when they should be exhaling. Nerissa, however, has learned to BREATHE OUT as she soars up into thin air, then down toward the water below. Some performers have problems letting go in the face of pressure. Not Nerissa. Fully *expressive,* she doesn't hold back, doesn't *de*press herself. She gives her all to her performance.

As she breathes out, she penetrates the surface of the water and, fully confident that she will rise again, Nerissa allows herself to plunge to the depths. She lets herself RIDE WITH that outgoing breath and that downward swirling of water that her dive has created.

COMPLETION

Nerissa enters the final, or "completion" phase of the ACT with a well-completed FOLLOW THROUGH. She maintains her form, poise, and commitment to the very end, fully extending her body from fingertips to toes. This part of her dive demonstrates her ability to *fulfill* what she has set out to accomplish.

At last she coils, bends, and lets herself BOUNCE BACK to the top. Whether or not this particular dive was her best, Nerissa *trusts* the process and *trusts* her Self. Whatever the outcome, she *trusts* that she will bounce back. She will dive again.

Nerissa now lets herself SOAK IN or assimilate what she has just done. She takes it all in—both the internal feedback from her body and mind, as well as the response of her coach, her friends and family, the judges, and the crowd. She is totally *aware*, basking in the glow of her accomplishment while taking note of what she might do to improve. This soaking-in time is her chance to refuel and recharge for her next dive, when a new act or cycle of energy commences.

Finally, Nerissa returns to the bench to REST FROM her activity. She clears her mind and thinks of nothing for a short time. It marks the end of the act. Nerissa recognizes that this temporary respite is essential to her continued peak performance. It is her time for *self-regeneration.*

●●●●●●●●●●●●●

After this short pause, Nerissa contemplates her next challenge. She reflects once again on the essence of why she's really here, what this journey is really all about. She remembers something her coach once told her: "Diving introduces yourself to your Self in mid-air." She knows this next dive is all-important, but instead of thinking about the points she needs and things she could have done better on her previous dives, she thinks about this joyful meeting with her Self in mid-air. The dive will be her greeting to her Self, the air and to the world. She will fly as no bird ever does, twisting and tumbling through space and time. In an instant the sky will become water, the water, sky. She envisions this dance. She will be ready for this next dive—this next act.

Clearly, Nerissa is a peak performer, a high achiever. Paradoxically, she is free to unleash her potential and perform at her best precisely because she's not overly concerned about her score.

Nerissa obviously wants to do well every step of the way, to execute perfect dives and win her medals. But these accomplishments are just part of a larger process. Nerissa is simply using her athletic prowess, her artistry, her sport to challenge herself—to draw upon and use all of herself, to express all of herself. By being fully alive in the moment, fully engaged in the process of performing optimally, she's able to excel—able to be at her best. Call her an artist with an athletic spirit or an athlete with an artistic spirit—either way Nerissa's the ultimate performer.

Remember the Scottish runner in the movie "Chariots of Fire"? A missionary who grew up in a religious family, he's asked by his disapproving sister why he runs. His answer: "Because when I run, I feel God's pleasure." That's how Nerissa feels when she is diving. Indeed, that is how any of us can feel when we're performing at our peak in whatever arena we choose. Most of us will never learn to soar beautifully off a high board, but the trick is to capture the spirit of the high diver and infuse it into our actions—not only the admirable grit of the athlete but the marvelous grace of the artist.

•••••••••••••

A successful act (such as a dive off a board) is an energy cycle and the basic unit of a longer achievement process (such as the winning of a Gold Medal). In the following chapter we describe how the effective management of our energy cycles promotes a "state of flow" and increases our chances of playing "in the zone."

8

FLOW

It happens. Sometimes in the course of play a moment arrives when an athlete experiences a quick and distinct shift of consciousness. Suddenly, performance is dramatically improved as the player becomes intensely focused—totally immersed in the challenge—and utterly confident of successful action. When this moment in time and space arrives, the athlete has entered into a *deep state of flow*, or what in sports is more commonly referred to as *the zon*e.

Typically the experience of being in the zone persists only a few seconds, but a well-trained athlete with a disciplined mind is capable of sustaining this optimal performance state for hours.

In his book, *Playing in the Zone*, Andrew Cooper includes numerous descriptions of the zone as provided by some of the athletes who've been there. Below are a few of these descriptions.

British golf pro, Tony Jacklin:

> *When I'm in this state, this cocoon of concentration, I'm living fully in the present, not moving out of it. I'm aware of every inch of my swing... I'm absolutely engaged, involved in what I'm doing at that particular moment. That's the important thing. That's the difficult state to arrive at.*

Former basketball star, Bill Russell:

Every so often a Celtic game would heat up so that it became more than a physical or even mental game, and would be magical. That feeling is difficult to describe, and I certainly never talked about it when I was playing. When it happened I could feel my play rise to a new level.... At that special level all sorts of odd things happened....It was almost as if we were playing in slow motion. During those spells I could almost sense how the next play would develop and where the next shot would be taken. Even before the other team brought the ball in bounds, I could feel it so keenly that I'd want to shout to my teammates, "It's coming there!"—except that I knew everything would change if I did. My premonitions would be consistently correct, and I always felt then that I not only knew all the Celtics by heart but also the opposing players, and that they all knew me. There have been many times in my career when I felt moved or joyful, but these were the moments when I had chills pulsing up and down my spine.

Tennis great, Billie Jean King:

It's a perfect combination of...violent action taking place in an atmosphere of total tranquility...When it happens I want to stop the match and grab the microphone and shout, "That's what it's all about." Because it is. It's not the big prize I'm going to win at the end of the match or anything else. It's just having done something that's totally pure and having experienced the perfect emotion, I'm always sad that I can't communicate that feeling right at the moment it's happening. I can only hope people realize what's going on.

Russian weight lifter, Yuri Vlasov:

At the peak of tremendous and victorious effort while the blood is pounding in your head, all suddenly becomes quiet within you. Everything seems clearer and whiter than ever before, as if great spotlights had been turned on.

> *...At that moment you have the conviction, that you contain all the power in the world, that you are capable of everything, that you have wings. There is no more precious moment in life than this, the white moment, and you will work very hard for years just to taste it again.*

Less magical—but more readily accessible than a *deep flow state* or a trip into *the zone*—is a state of consciousness referred to as *a flow experience.*

Musicians, artists, surgeons, lawyers, bricklayers—anyone can "get into the flow." It is mainly a matter of being totally focused—doing what one is doing. A leisurely walk through the woods on an autumn day may not be an ecstatic trip into the zone, but it certainly can be the ground for a pleasant and wonderful flow experience.

A flow experience comes pretty close to what John Dewey (1934) called simply *an* experience.

Here is what he wrote:

> *We have an experience when the material experienced runs its course to fulfillment. Then and only then is it integrated within and demarcated in the general stream of experience from other experiences. A piece of work is finished in a way that is satisfactory; a problem receives its solution; a game is played through; a situation, whether that of eating a meal, playing a game of chess, carrying on a conversation, writing a book, or taking part in a political campaign, is so rounded out that its close is a consummation and not a cessation.*
>
> *Such an experience is a whole and carries with it its own individualizing quality and self-sufficiency. It is an experience.*

My own personal experience in attempting to enhance performance by deliberately evoking states of flow came about in a rather circuitous way. Here's my story.

It was the spring of 1977, and I was fast approaching the mythic age of forty. That age sounds extremely young to me right now, but at the time I was feeling extremely old and lifeless—all traces of ambition and athleticism had drained from my body. My work was suffering, and I had forgotten how to play. Spiritually and emotionally I was distraught. Between marriages, I was wallowing in the middle of a mid-life crisis. I scarcely had the ambition and energy for a brisk walk, let alone any serious athletic pursuits.

While, generally speaking, my efforts toward getting back on track were woefully lacking, I did manage, however, to discipline myself to perform at least one constructive daily routine. Each day I took twenty to thirty minutes to sit and meditate.

I'd always been drawn to Eastern philosophies, but I got serious about developing a meditation practice after reading the works of Herbert Benson and others. A cardiologist and professor at the Harvard medical school, Dr. Benson presented a compelling argument that physical and emotional health could be improved without the use of drugs, by using a simple meditative technique that evoked a peaceful and balanced state of being that he referred to as the "Relaxation Response." He suggested that most of us could learn to deal more effectively with stress and inner tensions and that regardless of whether one was profoundly religious or a non-believer, it was useful to devote twenty minutes each day to systematically eliciting the Relaxation Response.

Benson's "system" is a very basic meditation technique. Mainly he suggests:

- *sit quietly in a comfortable position—*
- *pay attention to your breathing while silently saying the word "ONE" on your exhalations—*
- *maintain a passive attitude—not worrying about whether or not you're doing the technique correctly.*

Once I started meditating regularly, I became "positively addicted" to the daily routine. Drawing upon some earlier training in self-hypnosis, I experienced no difficulty in focusing my attention on the rhythms and patterns of my breathing. Paying attention to each inhalation and exhalation, I easily evoked a pleasant, lighthearted state of being and a distinct sense that these experiences would have a long-term positive impact on my health. Most of my friends and family considered what I was doing a little weird, but they were generally supportive, and when I would isolate myself somewhere to meditate, they'd refer to my absence as Alex being off *"doing his thing."*

With my daily meditations and resumption of some bicycling and swimming a few days a week, I experienced a gradual return of energy. But what I really felt I needed was a more vigorous and competitive athletic challenge.

Then one morning I got the call. It was from my younger brother, Don. He suggested that I join him in signing up for a seven-mile community "fun run."

In 1977, long distance running had not yet become a mainstream activity. In my mind only current and former track stars built like gazelles would sign up for such an enterprise. The idea of running a seven-mile course struck me as absurd, if not downright crazy.

I enjoyed sports of all kinds, played a lot of them reasonably well, and was in fairly good shape. But I'd never run more than a couple times around a track at any one time in life, and the thought of running—just running for seven straight miles—seemed like an invitation to a death march.

But after some discussion Don convinced me that the upcoming event would not be a highly competitive and overwhelming challenge. If you got tired, you walked, and most of the participants would just be interested in finishing, not racing. It would be a friendly community celebration of springtime with hundreds of people, young and old, participating.

After anguishing about it for a few days, I decided that I'd do it. I wrote out a check for the registration fee and mailed in the application form. I'd signed up for the big run that would take place in just six weeks.

I bought a pair of running shoes and felt some excitement about the upcoming event, but after three weeks of training, I had seriously considered abandoning the adventure. It wasn't fun, and even at a slow pace, I found that I'd have to quit after running fewer than three miles. The soles of my feet hurt, my knees creaked, and my ribs ached. How was I going to run seven miles with only three more weeks of training?

I took a couple of days off, and found that, during a particularly pleasant meditation session in which I was having a nice flow experience, I stayed focused on my breathing, but in my mind's eye I wasn't sitting cross-legged on a cushion. I was on the road. I was running. In my imagination my legs miraculously and painlessly carried me along, while my upper body sat there—spine erect, body centered—breathing in and breathing out, rhythmically and flowingly.

When I got back on the real road the next day, my attitude had changed dramatically. I didn't think of myself as confronting the arduous task of having to run a specific distance. Instead I saw myself as taking my breathing practice on the road with my focus on how much pleasant time I could spend moving along easily and flowingly.

My new attitude helped a lot. I moved along very slowly, but now at least the first twenty minutes of my runs became flow experiences, and gradually I was able to go longer and longer distances without my usual aches and pains.

On race day, I was a bit nervous because I still had not run more than four miles at any one time, and I wondered, since I'd significantly under-trained for a seven-mile run, whether I was foolishly setting myself up for some serious pain.

But soon after the run got underway, I fell into a nice breathing pattern, and my anxieties vanished. Brother Don and the front runners were soon way ahead of me, while I maintained a nice slow and easy nine-minute-mile pace, allowing myself to get caught up in the flow of hundreds of other people moving along the same path together at roughly the same speed. Time passed much more quickly and painlessly than I'd ever imagined, and soon I found myself in very unfamiliar territory, having reached the five-mile mark of the run. I was confident now that I'd actually complete the run and was even tempted to pick up my pace a bit. But not wanting this horse to come up lame, I kept to my slow and steady gait—stayed focused on my breathing—and eased my way to the finish line.

I was thrilled. I'd done it. For an experienced and talented runner, such an undertaking was just a warm-up, but for me it was a huge accomplishment.

As I walked about the grassy riverbed area near the finish line on this sunny spring day and mingled with the other finishers, I marveled at how bright, clear, and slowed-down everything looked to me as I reveled in the trance-like state that I'd experienced on the run.

Though this first experience didn't push me into a steady round of organized running events, I soon replaced my sitting meditation practice with daily runs.

My distances remained moderate, and I continued to run at a relatively slow pace, but gradually I was building my strength, and by the fall of 1981, I felt bold enough to sign up for a run called The Big Ten—a ten-mile run that wound its way around the streets of Ann Arbor and ended on the fifty-yard line of the University of Michigan football stadium. Seven miles was still the longest course I'd ever run, so this event would certainly present me with a new and interesting challenge.

It was a nice cool race day, and while it wasn't my custom to do so, I drank a large mug of black tea that morning, and the caffeine jacked me up into a more competitive spirit than usual. The beginning of the course along Main Street sloped downward somewhat, and taking advantage of that downward slope, I ran the first mile in six minutes, fifty-nine seconds.

For a serious runner, that's just a comfortable cruising-speed, but for me, it was flying. I was worried that I'd exhausted myself and would have to start walking, but to my delight I found I was able to maintain a nice steady pace. For the first time ever, I felt I wasn't just "doing" a run—I was really running.

I wasn't thirsty. I wasn't tired. I wasn't about to make any stops and start walking. I just wanted to stay with my breathing, stay with my horse—stay with the flow.

I did.

I'd slowed down to a seven-and-a-half minute-mile pace, but as I entered the tunnel leading onto the football field, I felt an extra boost of adrenaline and indulged myself in the fantasy of being a speedy running back on the U of M football squad, wearing the maize and blue and making a dash for the fifty-yard line.

Again finishing was a treat, and I truly enjoyed the feeling of having performed at my best. But flow experiences are wonderfully addictive, so within a few days, I found myself in search of a new running challenge.

Running a marathon didn't really appeal to me. I worried it might be too hard on my body and ultimately not the kind of sport to get into. But when I learned that the Detroit Marathon was to take place in a month, I signed up for it.

I assured myself that I wouldn't really have to finish the whole 26.2 mile course, but I figured I could run at least half of it, which would still be a long distance record for me, and by surrounding myself with top-performing athletes, I'd have a great chance at another optimal experience.

While I enjoyed the process of preparing for the marathon, I never pushed myself beyond a twelve-mile practice run. The night before the race I was suddenly hit with an overwhelming feeling that I had no business signing up for this event and that some sort of tragic outcome was bound to ensue.

My reactions surprised me. I felt fine at the pre-race conference/dinner with Billy Rogers of Boston Marathon fame as guest speaker, but soon after entering my hotel room at the Renaissance Center in downtown Detroit, I found myself extremely jittery.

After finally falling asleep, I kept awakening from a series of nightmares. In one dream, I am trying to run through wet cement. Finally my legs give out and, as I collapse near the corner of Kercheval and St. Jean I'm surrounded by a gang of young thugs who carry knives and glare menacingly at me.

In another dream, I've had a heart attack and I'm being carried away on a stretcher. A tall grim-looking doctor in a white coat is telling me that I had no business trying to run a marathon and he reprimands me for not having had my yearly physical exam and a stress test.

Early morning arrived too quickly after my fitful night and I felt groggy and rather disengaged as I boarded the bus for the short ride across the water to Ontario, Canada where the race would begin. But as the dense fog hovering over the Detroit River and the downtown streets was slowly swept away by a cool October breeze and a bright sun rose, my spirits lifted and I felt eager for the run to begin.

Being in the midst of the swarm of thousands of excited runners, I was easily moved along at the start of the race, and before long, we'd tunneled our way under the river from the Canadian border, back to U.S. soil.

When we emerged from the dim underworld to weave our way through the streets of Detroit, the skies turned blue, and all my heavy thoughts of an impending disaster dissipated into thin air.

Moving past the courthouse, the restaurants in Greektown and St. Mary's Church and then heading east on Jefferson Avenue, I maintained a slow, comfortable nine-minute-mile pace.

Distracted by the sights and sounds of the city streets, the chattering of the runners and comments from the crowds along the sidewalks, I stayed engaged in what I was doing, but wasn't really into my running in any particularly memorable way.

A little later as we were passing by the Chrysler plant, my legs started to tire, and I began to feel rather lethargic, but I lumbered along, resigned to the fact that I wouldn't be experiencing any *flow states* today. This run would be just a long, tedious haul. It was a Sunday, but I was at work. For many, Sunday was a day for worship and leisure time, but not for me. I had a job to do and I'd just muddle through it.

But as I approached the city limits at Alter Road and Jefferson, and continued on the route of the marathon into Grosse Pointe Park, I was moving into very familiar territory, and a novel sort of energy bubbled up from within as this silly event took on a whole new meaning for me.

After running for a couple hours, the mind can go a little wild, and I allowed myself to imagine that this marathon was the culmination of a heroic journey. Suddenly I was Odysseus. Having taken leave from the village where I was born and raised, I'd sought out new lands and new adventures. But now, after twenty years, I was returning home.

I'd been born and raised in Grosse Pointe Park, growing up in the old homestead at the corner of Audubon and Vernor, the house my grandma had built and where my brother and his family now lived. The house was located just a block from St. Clare of Montifalco Church and school, where I'd served as an altar boy and learned my lessons from the nuns through the eighth grade and where, with my family, I'd attended Mass on Sundays and Holy Days.

There were plenty of trees and parks and green space for play in our neighborhood, and scarcely a mile away lay Lake Saint Clair where we swam in the summer and skated in the winter.

My intense response to entering Grosse Pointe shouldn't have surprised me. Although my adult self had long ago said goodbye to this place as a community where I wanted to live, I couldn't deny the strong gravitational pull often felt for returning home. Perhaps the words of Bart Giamatti can help explain it:

> *Home is a concept, not a place; it is a state of mind where self-definition starts; it is origins—the mix of time and place and smell and weather wherein one first realizes one is an original, perhaps like others, especially those one loves, but discrete, distinct, not to be copied. Home is where one first learned to be separate and it remains in the mind as the place where reunion, if it ever were to occur, would happen.*

As I ran past Kensington and then Bedford, vivid memories of being young and exuberant and fleet of foot flooded my mind. I no longer felt tired and lethargic. By the time we'd passed the Veterans War Memorial building and Jefferson had turned into Lakeshore Drive, I'd picked up my pace and run farther than I ever had in my life.

I was into a nice state of flow at this point, and while being cheered from the sidelines, I suddenly noticed I was moving along side-by-side and step-by-step with a fellow marathoner—a lean, middle-aged black man. Our breathing patterns were clearly audible and had become synchronized as we trotted along together at precisely the same pace like a perfectly matched team of horses with no hint of rivalry—only a shared interest in arriving at a final destination.

Detroit had long been a hotbed of racial tensions and, in outlying areas such as Grosse Pointe, blacks and other minorities were not often welcomed, but on this particular day, all was right with the world, and harmony and goodwill prevailed everywhere as I, the Prodigal Son, accompanied by a black brother, returned home to a glorious reception.

The marathon proceeded farther east past St. Paul's Church, and when I stepped off the hard pavement to run for a brief stretch along the comfortable green grassy banks that lined the lakeshore, everything appeared divinely ordered. I felt the earth beneath my feet, the challenge of an oncoming westerly breeze, and enjoyed a wondrous scene on my right where bluish-green waves, interspersed with choppy whitecaps, rolled in from the freighter channel, and where, above the horizon against a mostly blue sky, a fiery white sun was shining. In harmony with the basic elements of the world—*fire, earth, air, water*, I found myself whispering the words of Gerard Manley Hopkins as I moved along effortlessly.

The world is charged with the grandeur of God.
It will flame out, like shining from shook foil...

Suddenly it occurred to me:

This is it. I have arrived. I'm in the zone!

People talk about having a momentary "near-death experience" (N.D.E.), wherein one's whole life suddenly passes before one's eyes. My experience was neither momentary nor deathly, but I saw my whole life pass before my eyes. It was a slow-motion, seven-minute, rapturously alive experience.

The lake triggered images from my youth as I visualized myself swimming and sailing there in the summer. And I recalled how in the winter the waters were magically transformed into a crystal sheet of glass, and I saw myself skating fast, the wind at my back.

Next came images of my young adult years, when I was a theology student struggling to understand what the universe had in store for me and striving to develop my spiritual life. It was a very different time in my life, but again

Hopkins' words came to mind and inspired me to fly like a bird, to buck the wind, keep my spirits alive, achieve mastery, and push onward to the completion of my journey.

I caught this morning morning's minion, king-
dom of daylight's dauphin, dapple-dawn-drawn Falcon, in his riding
Of the rolling level underneath him steady air, and striding...

In his ecstasy! Then off, off forth on swing,
As a skate's heel sweeps smooth on a bow-bend: the hurl and gliding
Rebuffed the big wind. My heart in hiding

Stirred for a bird—the achieve of, the mastery of the thing!
Brute beauty and valour and act, oh, air, pride, plume here...

No wonder of it: sheer plod makes plough down sillion
Shine, and blue-bleak embers, ah my dear,
Fall, gall-themselves, and gash gold-vermillion.

As the route of the marathon made the turn off Lakeshore Drive to Kercheval—to circle back toward Detroit—I maintained my pace, but I was struggling. No longer in the zone, I had peaked.

By the corner of Audubon and Kercheval, just one block from the old homestead, I was close to the eighteen-mile mark of the marathon. Having made it that far, I decided I could and would make the finish line at Belle Isle. I pushed onward.

At the twenty-mile marker, however, I hit the proverbial "wall." My spirit was willing to rise above it, but my legs had given out on me. I decided then and there that marathon running was not for me. Sprints and middle-distance runs would serve me better as a means of mobilizing energy and staying in shape.

With the exception of a last-minute run to the finish line, all I could manage in that final stretch of the marathon was a painfully slow walk. But, while the adventure could've been more pleasurable—and glamorously successful—I couldn't complain about a journey that had provided me with those unforgettable seven minutes in paradise.

In retrospect, I don't believe hitting the wall was inevitable. What I was lacking at the time was the running method Danny Dreyer describes in his book *Chi Running*. The author teaches a highly energy-efficient technique that involves running with a full-body tilt—leaning from the ankles and engaging the forward pull of gravity. The technique likely would have helped me avoid hitting the wall. While my pace no doubt would've slowed from the speed I'd maintained during the middle of the run, I'm convinced that Dryer's technique would've spared my legs, thus enabling me to sustain a leisurely cruise to the finish line.

Evoking a "nice state of flow" while playing a sport is a relatively simple matter. Getting into *the zone* is considerably more complicated. The conditions need to be just right. But, even if it happens only once in a lifetime, it's marvelous to be in top form, to fall into a *deep* flow state and to experience the squeezing out of every drop of one's potential. While it may be a rare occurrence, it's wonderful to have that experience stored in one's memory bank. A peak-performing experience offers us a sense of identity and reminds us of our capacities. In times of doubt and low self-confidence, it can be reassuring to reflect on those moments of high performance.

Uneasiness with the unknown is perhaps the primary reason athletes do not more often allow themselves to fall into a deep flow state. If a performer isn't ready for the zone, it can be shocking to find oneself suddenly in a world where everything is in sharp focus, where colors are unusually vivid, and where suddenly things happening at great speed appear to progress in slow motion. While some may immediately welcome it as wonderfully magical and mystical, others may find the experience scary or weird and wonder whether their Gatorade has been spiked with a psychedelic drug.

Associated with that discomfort with the unknown is what psychologists refer to as a performer's *"upper-limits"* problem. Some athletes become satisfied and accustomed to performing at a certain level and conclude that this degree of excellence is all they can expect and all they deserve. They are uneasy about the possibility of dramatically raising their level of play and having a peak-performing experience. Unconsciously they sabotage themselves. They avoid the zone.

A change of perception can be very helpful. If an athlete can regard the zone as his natural right and a wonderful and safe place to go, and if he can ease up and not over-control himself, he is more likely to get there. Access to a deep flow state involves a surrendering of the self, as the performer (without the use of drugs) slips into an altered state of consciousness—an extra-ordinary state. In this state the performer is highly alert and aware, and if it feels odd or crazy, it's only because this psychological state is new and different.

While some athletes avoid the zone, others seek it out and orchestrate their way into it with pre-game rituals and techniques drawn from a wide variety of disciplines and practices—psychology, religion, mythology, meditation, poetry, music, dance.

•••••••••••••

A sports activity will never guarantee a flow experience, or a spiritual awakening, or a trip into the zone. But an athlete can take steps that will increase his or her chances of evoking a flow experience while playing a sport. The trick is to set challenges for oneself that are neither too difficult nor too easy, and then simply to permit oneself to become totally absorbed in the activity, simultaneously maintaining focus and managing consciousness. It again boils down to accessing all 12 Powers of the Energy Cycle and gaining mastery of the self. In the chapters that follow, we focus on developing and mastering the 12 Powers.

9

Test Yourself

A first step toward mastery can begin with a heightened awareness of how you are currently doing.

In this chapter you'll find an inventory for assessing your present levels of competency in relation to each of the 12 Powers. Apart from the usefulness of determining your score, the very process of examining yourself is inherently beneficial in that you become more keenly aware of what you *typically do* before, during, and after your performance of an individual athletic act.

While taking this inventory, it's useful to have in mind the sport or athletic activity that you engage in most frequently, or that you play most intensely. For example, if you golf regularly and are a rather serious student of the game, but play other sports only occasionally, you should always keep your golf game in mind, not some other sport, when responding to the statements below.

Think about your style of play or how you practice your sport and then, next to each line item below, assign the scale number (from 1 to 9) that best describes the extent to which you agree with the statement.

Very Strongly Disagree	Strongly Disagree	Somewhat Disagree	Disagree	Neither Agree nor Disagree	Somewhat Agree	Agree	Strongly Agree	Very Strongly Agree
1	2	3	4	5	6	7	8	9

1. Fire up

_______ a. I am highly motivated to perform at my best.

_______ b. I always have the passion and desire to perform at my best.

_______ c. I "fire up" for the task at hand.

_______ d. Even if I am physically and mentally exhausted, I dig deep within myself and pump myself up for the task at hand.

_______ e. I burn with desire to perform maximally.

[ ] **Total Score for #1 Fire up**

Very Strongly Disagree	Strongly Disagree	Somewhat Disagree	Disagree	Neither Agree nor Disagree	Somewhat Agree	Agree	Strongly Agree	Very Strongly Agree
1	2	3	4	5	6	7	8	9

2. Settle down

_______ a. Even when the performance situation is intense, I find a quiet spot within me and put myself at ease.

_______ b. No matter how exciting the play gets, I am always able to settle myself down and maintain my poise.

_______ c. No matter how intense the performance situation, I stay in control of my emotions.

_______ d. I keep my composure, staying calm and collected when engaged in athletic activity.

_______ e. However challenging the situation may be, I remain in my "comfort zone" and perform at my best.

[ ] **Total Score for #2 Settle down**

Very Strongly Disagree	Strongly Disagree	Somewhat Disagree	Disagree	Neither Agree nor Disagree	Somewhat Agree	Agree	Strongly Agree	Very Strongly Agree
1	2	3	4	5	6	7	8	9

3. Aim at

______ a. When I step onto the playing field, I know what I want to accomplish.

______ b. I am a very goal-oriented performer.

______ c. I am always clear and precise about my goals/objectives in a game situation.

______ d. In most endeavors, I am self-directed and readily identify my goal/purpose.

______ e. Whether practicing or in a game situation, I target my objectives and have a clear idea of what I want and need to do.

☐ **Total Score for #3 Aim at**

Very Strongly Disagree	Strongly Disagree	Somewhat Disagree	Disagree	Neither Agree nor Disagree	Somewhat Agree	Agree	Strongly Agree	Very Strongly Agree
1	2	3	4	5	6	7	8	9

4. Sense inside

______ a. Before performing an athletic act, it is easy for me to go into my head and—like in a dream or movie—to see myself doing it.

______ b. As I am getting ready to execute an athletic act, I get a good sense of what that act is going to feel like when I actually do it.

______ c. Once I know what I want to accomplish, I guide myself into a deeply felt sense of achieving my goal.

______ d. Before moving toward a desired goal, I get a deeply felt positive sense or a "picture" of myself reaching that desired goal.

______ e. In preparing myself for an athletic act, I frequently get a good feeling or a clear visualization of myself performing that act.

☐ **Total Score for #4 Sense inside**

Very Strongly Disagree	Strongly Disagree	Somewhat Disagree	Disagree	Neither Agree nor Disagree	Somewhat Agree	Agree	Strongly Agree	Very Strongly Agree
1	2	3	4	5	6	7	8	9

5. Go for

_______ a. I encourage myself to take calculated risks.

_______ b. Once I get a sense that I am fully prepared for what I want to do, I don't hesitate—I take the leap.

_______ c. I tend to spring forward into action—decisively and definitively.

_______ d. I welcome challenges and encourage myself to "go for it."

_______ e. I'm not overly cautious or tentative in my play.

[ ] **Total Score for #5 Go for**

Very Strongly Disagree	Strongly Disagree	Somewhat Disagree	Disagree	Neither Agree nor Disagree	Somewhat Agree	Agree	Strongly Agree	Very Strongly Agree
1	2	3	4	5	6	7	8	9

6. Focus on

_______a. I keep my head in the game—and stay focused on the task at hand.

_______b. When I play a game, I focus intensely.

_______c. When I perform an athletic act, I concentrate fully and do not permit my mind to wander.

_______d. I'm not sidetracked when I attempt to get something accomplished.

_______e. I'm very self-disciplined and not easily distracted.

[ ] **Total Score for #6 Focus on**

Very Strongly Disagree	Strongly Disagree	Somewhat Disagree	Disagree	Neither Agree nor Disagree	Somewhat Agree	Agree	Strongly Agree	Very Strongly Agree
1	2	3	4	5	6	7	8	9

7. Breathe out

_______a. When I do something, I give my all, holding nothing back.

_______b. Once I start moving toward my goal, I go all out to achieve that goal.

_______c. When I play, I tend to fully exert myself and "go all out."

_______d. My playing style tends to be free-flowing and unrestrained.

_______e. When I perform an athletic act, I give my utmost.

[ ] **Total Score for #7 Breathe out**

Very Strongly Disagree	Strongly Disagree	Somewhat Disagree	Disagree	Neither Agree nor Disagree	Somewhat Agree	Agree	Strongly Agree	Very Strongly Agree
1	2	3	4	5	6	7	8	9

8. Ride with

_______a. I frequently feel that the momentum of the play is on my side and all I really have to do is "ride the energy" to perform at my best.

_______b. Once I get on a roll, I give in to the feeling that everything will work out in my favor.

_______c. It is easy for me to relinquish my sense of control and "just let it happen."

_______d. I tend to let myself loose and just "go with the flow."

_______e. I readily harmonize and synchronize my energies with the energies of a partner or other members of a team.

[ ] **Total Score for #8 Ride with**

Very Strongly Disagree	Strongly Disagree	Somewhat Disagree	Disagree	Neither Agree nor Disagree	Somewhat Agree	Agree	Strongly Agree	Very Strongly Agree
1	2	3	4	5	6	7	8	9

9. Follow through

_______a. Win or lose, I am a strong finisher and never give up.

_______b. As I move toward the completion of a goal, nothing holds me back from fully completing that goal.

_______c. When I wish to complete a goal, I follow through and fulfill that wish.

_______d. Once my goal is in sight, nothing stops me from completing my task.

_______e. I fully finish what I set out to do.

☐ **Total Score for #9 Follow through**

Very Strongly Disagree	Strongly Disagree	Somewhat Disagree	Disagree	Neither Agree nor Disagree	Somewhat Agree	Agree	Strongly Agree	Very Strongly Agree
1	2	3	4	5	6	7	8	9

10. Bounce back

_______a. I readily bounce back when I make a mistake or have a streak of bad luck.

_______b. Whether I am performing poorly or exceptionally well, my emotional reactions to my performance stay pretty much neutral or even-keeled.

_______c. Whatever happens on the playing field, I always trust that I'll recover.

_______d. In a game situation, I am neither way up nor way down—I maintain my balance and stay "centered."

_______e. I am quick to shrug off performance mistakes and get my play back on track.

☐ **Total Score for #10 Bounce back**

Very Strongly Disagree	Strongly Disagree	Somewhat Disagree	Disagree	Neither Agree nor Disagree	Somewhat Agree	Agree	Strongly Agree	Very Strongly Agree
1	2	3	4	5	6	7	8	9

11. Soak in

_______a. I welcome critiques and feedback on my performance.

_______b. I savor my accomplishments.

_______c. I tend to be very self-reflective, thinking about what I did well and about how I might improve.

_______d. After completing an athletic task, I review my performance, taking note of my shortcomings and welcoming critiques on my play.

_______e. After completing a successful performance, I make a point of reflecting on that performance and recalling in detail how it felt.

☐ **Total Score for #11 Soak in**

Very Strongly Disagree	Strongly Disagree	Somewhat Disagree	Disagree	Neither Agree nor Disagree	Somewhat Agree	Agree	Strongly Agree	Very Strongly Agree
1	2	3	4	5	6	7	8	9

12. Rest from

_______a. I can readily restore my energies with a quick (20-min. or less) power nap.

_______b. I have no trouble slowing down and relaxing after exerting myself on the playing field.

_______c. I like being on the go, but it's never difficult for me to slow down and rest.

_______d. When I get tired, I find I can readily regenerate my energies and renew myself by resting.

_______e. When I'm tired after a performance, I can fall asleep or rest deeply most anywhere (e.g. bus, plane, a lounge chair)

☐ **Total Score for #12 Rest from**

Create a personal profile of your Total Scores (▭) for each of the 12 Powers by plotting them on the graph below.

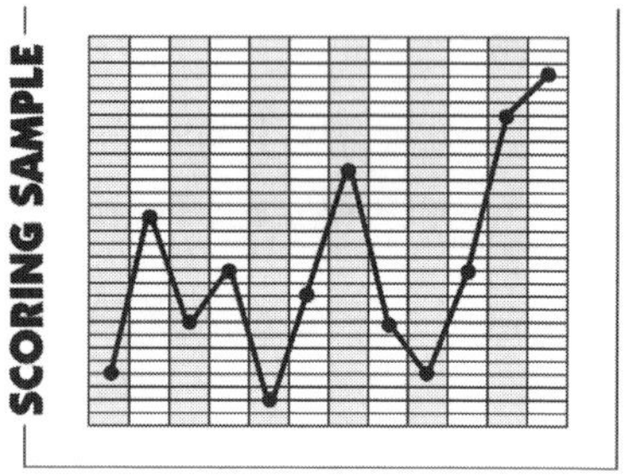

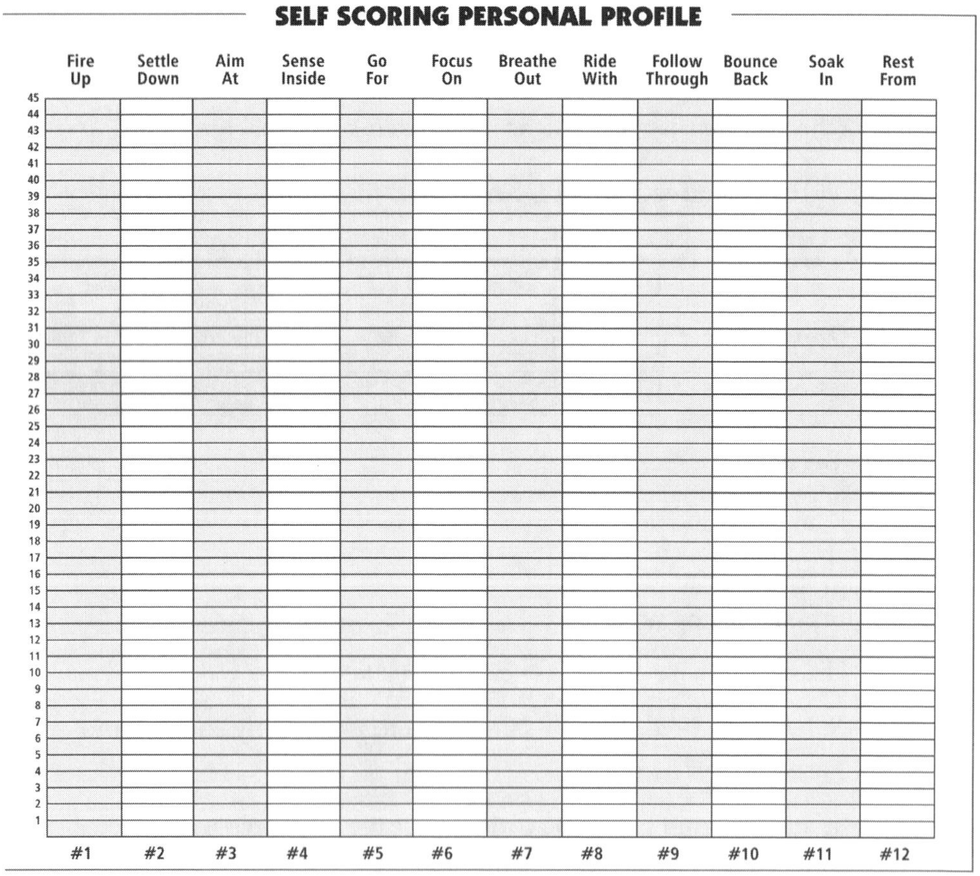

As you review your scores, bear in mind that they do not reflect enduring characteristic behavioral traits that cannot and will not change. Rather, your self-evaluations are "snapshots in time" of how you are currently doing. Think of a high score as a strength that can be developed. A low score, on the other hand, should be perceived, not as a weakness, but rather as a "developmental opportunity."

In another month or two, you may want to test yourself again. Check yourself out. See where you are.

As the ancient Greek philosopher, Thales, urges us:

> *"Know thyself."*
>
> —Inscription on the oracle-shrine of Apollo at Delphi, 6th century B.C.

10

PRACTICE

practice v. *1. to do or perform habitually or customarily; to make a habit of*
2. to perform or work at repeatedly so as to become proficient

How do you develop the 12 Powers of Self-Mastery? *Practice! Practice! Practice!*

It's always wonderful to watch a gifted athlete in action, executing powerful and magical moves that appear to flow naturally. But what most of us know is that those moves were not magically acquired. Like a black-belted martial artist or a professional ballet dancer, the athlete first isolated the moves, then developed and perfected them through daily exercises, repetitions, and routines. He weaves together a masterful performance, because he takes time to practice his individual moves—step by step, one by one—over and over.

Though the 12 Powers of the Energy Cycle should be grasped as a whole and developed mainly by using them on the playing fields and in the heat of battle, it can also be useful to step aside from the battlefield and practice the individual powers one at a time—consciously and deliberately.

In attempting to perform at one's best, one often discovers that the body and mind are at odds with each other. Among the practice activities on the following pages are yoga-like postures and exercises designed to align the body and mind while giving full and honest expression to each of the 12 individual powers. In these practices, the bones, the muscles, and the brain simultaneously express the same intent. As an athlete practices an individual power with total attention and the energies of the body and mind are fully coordinated and integrated, he or she begins truly to understand and possess that power.

Some of the activities listed below are sport-related and designed to take place on the playing fields, whereas others are designed to be practiced in the ordinary rooms and surroundings of your everyday life.

Do them! Then make up some of your own. One by one—practice each of the twelve individual powers.

The Victor

Developing Your #1 Power

Fire up—self-motivation

Starting any activity or task requires readily accessible energy. At the heart of this power is the ability to motivate your self. It's the capacity to become energized and enthusiastic—charged up for the task at hand. It's your ability to light a fire under yourself. Everyone gets tired and sluggish from time to time, but the performer with a highly developed number one capacity is almost invariably able to dig within himself and find the fire power to excel.

There are many ways to get yourself into a *"fired up"* state of being—ways to isolate and stimulate your #1 Power. Begin by understanding and practicing the following yoga-like pose.

The Victor

At the "fire up" stage of the Energy Cycle, you are preparing yourself for a victory. To get the juices flowing, it's helpful to mimic the jubilant pose of the victorious athlete. Think of yourself as having *already* attained a victory as you spring to your feet and jump for joy in celebration of a deeply desired win.

This pose reflects the abundant energy of a performer who's highly excited, wonderfully alive, and fully charged for the task at hand.

1. Stand up tall.
2. Get up on your toes and the balls of your feet.
3. Forming a V-shape, raise your arms and hands as high up over your head as possible.
4. Stretch out your fingers and the palms of your hands.
5. With vigorous exhalations, hear yourself exclaiming: *"Yes! Yes! Yes!"*
6. Sense yourself as totally alive and fully fired for the task at hand.

Other *practices/processes/exercises* for developing your #1 power:

1. Go to bed early. Get an extra two or three hours of sleep. Get up slowly. Stretch and groan like a powerful lion getting out of his den. Tell your Self that you're well rested, fully energized, and ready to *"seize the day."* Then do it. Get on with it, and don't look back.

2. Word play: write down on a 3x5 card key words associated with the number one power: *passion, energy, excitement, love, spark, charged, fired up, motivated, on fire*. Single out one of these words and repeat it over and over to yourself. Live with that word the whole day, or for at least five minutes straight. Let that word sink into your body and mind and energize you, penetrating your consciousness and influencing what you do and how you feel—and how and what you think. When you finish immersing your Self in one of the words on your list, go on to the next word.

3. Take a cold shower. Step out onto the bath mat and gently but briskly slap yourself all over your wet body. Look into the mirror and say out loud: "*Today I have all the power and energy I need to do what I want to do!*" Convince yourself that what you're saying is actually true, then get on with your next act of the day.

4. Grab a bright colored grapefruit or navel orange. Imagine that it's a miniature sun bursting with energy. Peel it and eat it slowly, embracing the notion that it's supplying you with unlimited fuel for the day.

5. Get yourself off the couch and take a stance in the middle of the room. Imagine you're in a boxing ring just before a big fight. Jump up and down on one leg, then the other. Make a fist and jab the air, panting and growling and hollering out loud. *Haaaah! Haaah! Pow! Pow!*

6. Find and read self-motivating quotations, such as this one:

"You must concentrate upon and consecrate yourself wholly to each day as though a fire were raging in your hair."
—Ancient Samurai Master

Write this quotation on a 'post it' and stick it somewhere that you'll see it and read it often.

7. Imagine yourself burning with passion for the thing you want to do. Say to yourself: *"Yes! Yes! Yes! I need...I want... I desire...I deserve...I am excited...I have the energy do it!"*

8. Sign up for a dance, yoga, or martial arts class. Let your main focus be on allowing the exercises and practices to refresh, stimulate, and energize you.

9. Throw yourself into performance situations and welcome all feelings of excitation, even in the form of butterflies or nervous tension. Just think of them positively, as indications of energy and adrenaline flow.

10. Play vibrant music with a good strong uplifting rhythm and beat—classic, rock, folk, whatever. Allow the music to move you, shake you. Let yourself dance.

11. Drink a lot of water. Eat a lot of fruits and vegetables. Exercise. Stretch. Breathe deeply. Be determined to feel vigorous. Choose to have all the power and energy you need to do what you need to do. Decide that it's so. Be fully energized.

12. Power #1 is your ability to say: *YES!* Say YES ten times in a row. YES YES YES YES YES YES YES YES YES YES! Say YES with a clenched fist. Jump for joy and say YES. Say YES with fire dancing in your eyes.

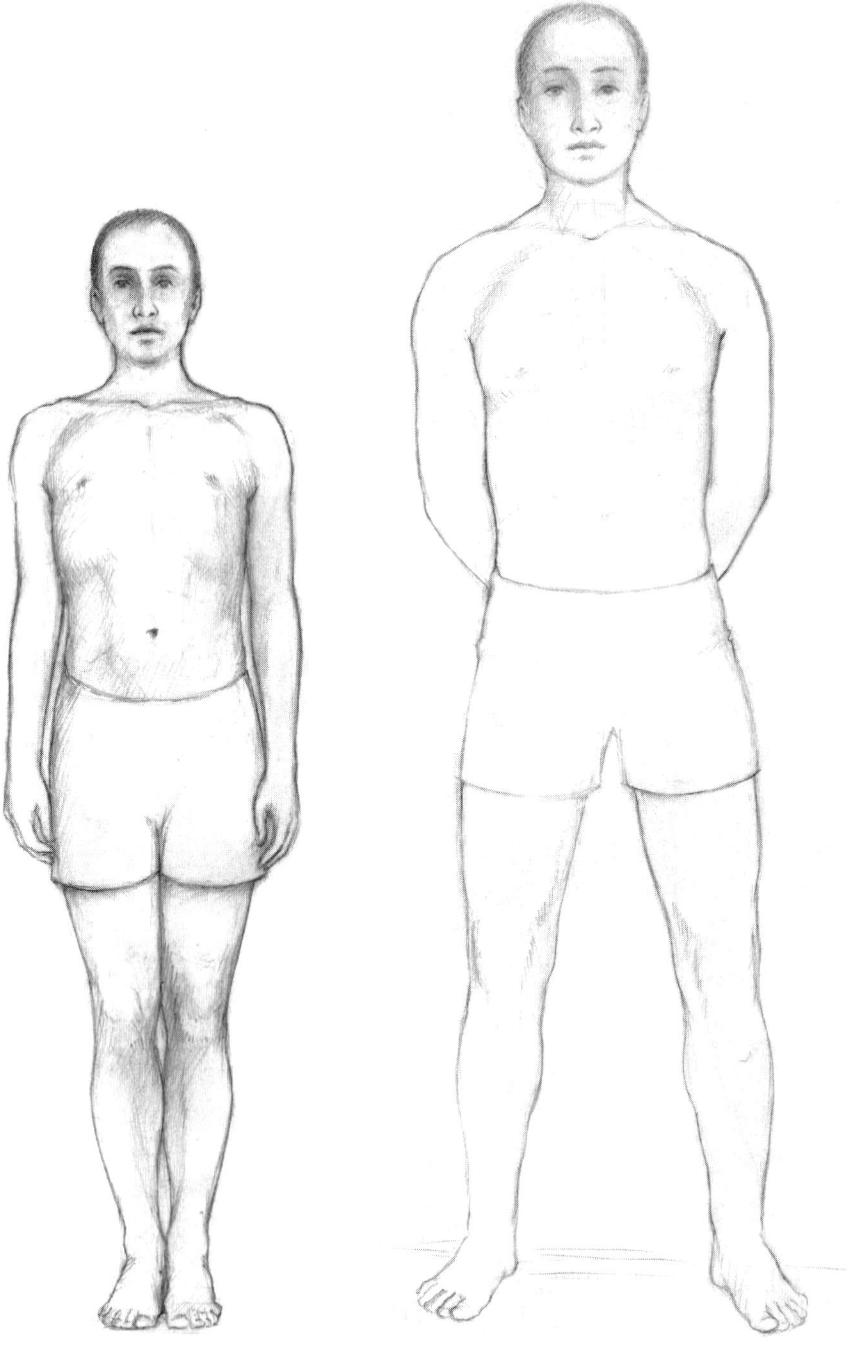

At Ease

Developing your #2 power

Settle down—self-control

Raw energy alone will not lead to accomplishment. To prepare for effective action, you must also harness and channel that energy. You must take command. Too much energy that isn't adequately settled down manifests itself as nervousness and an inability to undertake an activity with a comfortable sense of control. The person with a well-developed ability to settle down feels secure and enjoys the firm footing necessary to move into action calmly and efficiently.

By practicing this power, you prepare your self to step up and perform when you're called upon to do so. You learn to gain instant control of your self and not to be overwhelmed by your excitation. Begin by understanding and practicing the following yoga-like pose.

The 'At Ease' Pose

Here you stand in sharp contrast to the stiff, uptight, wooden-like soldier at his military post. In the 'at ease' posture, your attitude is casual and your breathing is relaxed. Your center of gravity lowers, and your legs grow steady and stable with your knees *not* locked and *not* bent.

1. Begin with your feet together, knees locked, and standing up as tall and upright as possible.

2. Hold your breath for the count of ten.

3. With a cleansing exhalation, spread your feet shoulder-width apart, unlock your knees, and lower your center of gravity.

4. Like a well-rooted tree, send your energy downward into the ground and allow yourself to sway slightly from side to side.

5. Clasp your hands lightly behind your back, and just stand there, comfortable, settled—breathing from your center.

Other practices/processes/exercises for developing your #2 power:

1. Stand comfortably with your feet shoulder-width apart and your knees not locked and not bent. In each hand hold a 5 to 20-pound barbell (choosing a weight size that is not overly strenuous). Gently twist, twirl and sway from side to side. Feel the strength and stability in your legs as you allow the weights that you are holding to help channel all your energy downward—into your thighs, knees, calves, ankles, feet, toes.

2. Imitate the moves and rituals of a major league baseball player as you step into the batter's box and assume a good firm stance. Dig in. Paw the ground. Shuffle your feet. Sink down. Shift your weight from foot to foot. Channel all your energy downward, into your thighs, knees, calves, ankles, feet, toes. Imagine yourself feeling totally secure and grounded—excited, but not a bit nervous. In total command.

3. Put yourself in an imaginary boxing ring and imitate the dance and catlike steps of a ferocious fighter circling his opponent. Crouch low. Breathe out. Breathe in. Pant a bit. Let your arms move a little, but focus all your energy on your legs and feet as you quickly shift your weight from side to side, moving into position for the big punch. Feel tough and invincible. In total control.

4. Sit on a bench, spine erect, feet planted firmly on the ground, your hands on your thighs. Breathe from your diaphragm and follow your breath as you inhale and exhale while engaging in some 'self-talk'—e.g. "I am a rock. I belong here. I deserve to be here. I can handle the task before me. I am in command."

5. Take a class or a few private lessons in a martial art. Learn how to *"ground"* and *"center"* yourself. Develop your ability to direct your energy downward. Ask the instructor to explain the concept.

6. Ask yourself: "How would I help a nervous kid or an over-excited puppy *settle down or gain control?*" Find the answer. Now do it! Help yourself get in control and settle down.

7. Imitate an ape. Swoop down low. Swing your arms from side to side. Scoop the earth. Ground yourself.

8. Taking a morning shower can be energizing. The ritual can also be a way to help give you a sense of being grounded. Experience the flow of the water as a gentle force that helps move your energy from the top of your head, down into your legs, and finally to the bottom of your feet. Allow the feel and sound of the water to put you into a trance-like state. From that relaxed and grounded position see and feel yourself performing those perfect athletic acts of your dreams.

9. Sometimes the act you are about to perform (e.g., giving a speech or making an important putt) may evoke an oversupply of adrenaline that makes you nervous and jumpy. When this happens, think of your body as an overly-excited and frisky horse that you need to settle down. Soothe yourself with calming words:

   Whoa! Whoa! Whoa! Easy does it.

10. Word play: *settled, at ease, in control, stable, secure, grounded.*

The Archer

Developing your #3 power

Aim at—self-direction

Optimal performers target their goals. Individuals with an underdeveloped capacity to "aim at" have trouble being clear about what they want. They move into action ill-prepared because they are guided only by vague notions about what they hope to accomplish.

Your development of this power can begin with the practice and understanding of the following yoga-like pose.

The Archer

The *archer* is a perfectly sculpted posture for expressing the total alignment of the body and mind as you direct yourself toward the attainment of a specific goal. While you hold this pose, direct your attention to a small target in the distance. From your relaxed and steady stance, feel fully confident of your capacity to keep your arrow pointing in the right direction and to hit your mark.

1. Place left foot forward, right foot back. Stand comfortably, your weight distributed evenly.

2. Drop into a crouch and place your body at a right angle to the target you are aiming at.

3. Imagine yourself holding a bow and drawing back the arrow with your right hand.

4. Breathing deeply and rhythmically, hold your stance as you gaze at your target.

5. Get the sense that your body and mind are totally aligned and that you will certainly hit your mark.

6. Repeat the above exercise—stretching the other side of the body by placing the *right* foot forward and drawing back the arrow with the *left* hand.

Other practices/processes/exercises for developing your #3 power:

1. There's something nice about going out for a walk or a run and deliberately not deciding beforehand where you'll be going and how long you'll be out. But just for practice, just as a way of developing your #3 Power, take a walk or a run with a definite timetable and set of goals in mind: e.g. "Today I will leave the house at 7:15 A.M. on the dot—run to the river and back, at the rate of nine minutes per mile and return to the house and stretch for seven minutes, then into the shower not later than 8:00 A.M."

2. Direct your attention to these words: *goal, objective, destination, result, direction, target, aim, achievement, accomplishment.*

3. In whatever you do today, question the direction of your action. Ask yourself: *Where am I headed? What's my goal? What's my desired anticipated outcome? What do I want to accomplish? What's my target? What am I aiming at?*

4. Practice being absolutely clear about what you want to accomplish. Every hour on the hour—for a whole day, remind yourself: *Clarity is power!*

5. Ask yourself: "What am I gravitating toward today? What's drawing me? What's my passion? What target wants me?"

6. Study and become fascinated with maps.

7. Be an arrow. Point yourself. Be the hood ornament on a '52 Mercury.

8. Become a goal-oriented person. Aim high and challenge yourself, but don't overreach. You are more likely to achieve a goal if you are specific in setting it and if you write it down. We should not be surprised by the following report from The Association for the Advancement of Applied Sport Psychology (AAASP):

"Research on athletes and in business psychology clearly indicates that people who set goals, and then periodically evaluate their goals, are more successful than people who do not set goals."

9. Focus your goals on performance rather than on results, allowing yourself to become highly motivated by a deep and personal sense of mission. Write out your mission statements.

   In his book, *Peak Performance, Mental Training Techniques of the World's Greatest Athletes,* Charles Garfield defines a mission statement and distinguishes it from a goal statement:

   The mission statement is a summation of your personal philosophy. What are your private reasons *for wanting to accomplish a special goal in your sport? This personal,* subjective *statement should be distinguished from the goal itself, which is an* objective *statement about a specific athletic achievement and can be quantitatively measured. For example, you might train to run a marathon and have as your mission statement " I want that incredible feeling of really being in command of myself that I get from pushing my body to the outer limits." The goal statement of the same mission might be "To run 26 miles and finish in the top 100."*

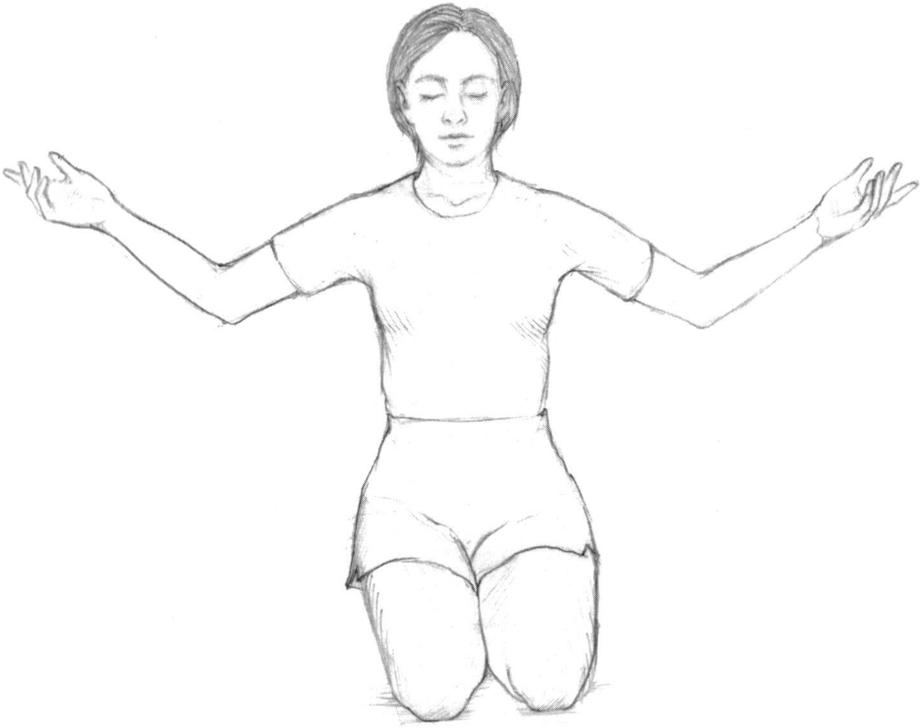

The Dreamer

Developing your #4 power

Sense inside—self-guidance

Keen awareness is the hallmark of this power. Here you continue the process of directing and guiding your attention and intention towards an increasingly well-defined goal. Sensing inside primarily involves heightened consciousness of how and what you see, hear, and feel as you create your *instant pre-play* of what you are about to accomplish. Individuals who have difficulty with this stage often experience doubt or mild confusion, rather than a clear sense of their readiness.

Begin development of your #4 power.

The Dreamer

As you lower your body into a kneeling position and close your eyes, you facilitate the process of turning inward and creating a dream-like state of mind. In this supplicant's pose, body and mind are aligned in the act of "praying" for the right thing to happen. This pose will help you evoke images of successful action and give you a deeply felt sense of what you hope to accomplish.

1. Kneel down. Rest your weight on your heels.
2. Close your eyes and extend your arms outward with the palms of your hands facing up.
3. Draw your elbows in toward each other, creating a gentle stretch in your back and shoulders.
4. Breathe slowly and deeply, your chin tucked inward, as if at attention.
5. As you follow your breath and feel the beat of your heart, get a deeply felt sense of what you hope to accomplish.
6. Let your mind be entertained by clear, precise images of yourself reaching specific goals and performing at your best.

Other practices/processes/exercises for developing your #4 power:

1. Immerse yourself in the spirit and meaning of these words one by one: *vision, dream, imagination, picture, view, deep felt sense, instant pre-play, gut feeling, inward knowing, self-guidance.*

2. Lie on the ground or sit upright in a chair with your hands clasped over your abdomen. Breathe in, breathe out. Close your eyes. Now guide your mind, imagining yourself performing an athletic act of some kind. Notice every detail. Where do you begin? What are you wearing? What color are your shoes? What are you touching? Where are you headed? How are you moving? How do you feel? What's the smell? What do you hear? What's the taste in your mouth? What do you want to accomplish? What's your dream? How does it end?

3. It has been said that the natural tendency of humankind is to hope vaguely and dread precisely. But if we have the capacity to be precise about what we dread, we can use that basic capacity and direct it more positively. We can develop our power to be precise in what we hope for. Spend a day dreaming your dreams and practicing your capacity *to be vivid and precise about what you hope to accomplish—what you wish to have happen.*

4. Close your eyes. Place your hands over your face and get in touch with your breathing and your heartbeat. Recall a melody. In your mind, play out a simple and memorable tune, such as, "Twinkle, Twinkle Little Star." Don't hum it or mouth it—just go inward and hear and feel its rhythm and beat. See, hear, and feel the first three notes of "Beethoven's Fifth Symphony."

5. Choose an ordinary activity such as eating a meal and become exceedingly aware of the *sensations* the experience triggers. While eating very slowly and in silence, notice what happens inwardly as you attend to every little detail: the feel and sight of the bright yellow lemon that you just cut in half and are about to squeeze onto your salmon steak, the feel of the warm bread on your fingertips, the aroma of the sauce, the taste and texture of the red tomato.

6. Get a couple of sheets of blank white paper and a good pen with nice ink flow, preferably a fountain pen. At the top of the first page jot down this statement: *I have a goal that I want to accomplish, and this is how I will look and feel as I perform at my best and reach that goal.* Without stopping to think, just let the hand that grasps the pen move. Let the pen "automatically" transcribe images and feelings of the performer who dwells within you. Let the pen reveal your heart and your head. Allow your writing to be a prediction of your upcoming positive performance.

7. While practicing a sport such as tennis, set aside time when you drop all thought about how you are performing and instead turn all your attention to the details of the racket you hold in your hand. Snap the strings. Listen to the ping. Smell the leather handle. Study the logo and the racket's overall design. And now from the feel of the racket and the sensations you detect on your fingertips, turn your attention inward to the feel of your heartstrings and the sound of your breathing. Then, maintaining your attention to detail, stroke the ball with increased awareness.

8. Experience your magical power for tricking the mind into seeing, hearing, tasting, feeling, touching, smelling things that in reality are not present to you. Do the following exercise:

   Relax. Close your eyes. Take yourself back in time and space to a memorable house that you once lived in or frequently visited. Open the front door. Imagine yourself walking slowly through each room of the house. What do you notice? Can you recall the colors? Can you touch the furniture? Do you see the light coming in through the various windows? Do you hear music playing and people talking? Can you recognize some friends or family members? Go into the kitchen. Can you get a smell and taste of something freshly baked?

   Pour yourself a glass of water. Open the refrigerator. Pull out a tray of ice. Hear the crackling. Feel the numbing cold on your fingertips as you grasp a couple of cubes and then hear them plunk into your glass of water. Continue your journey through the house. What do you see, hear, taste, feel, touch, smell?

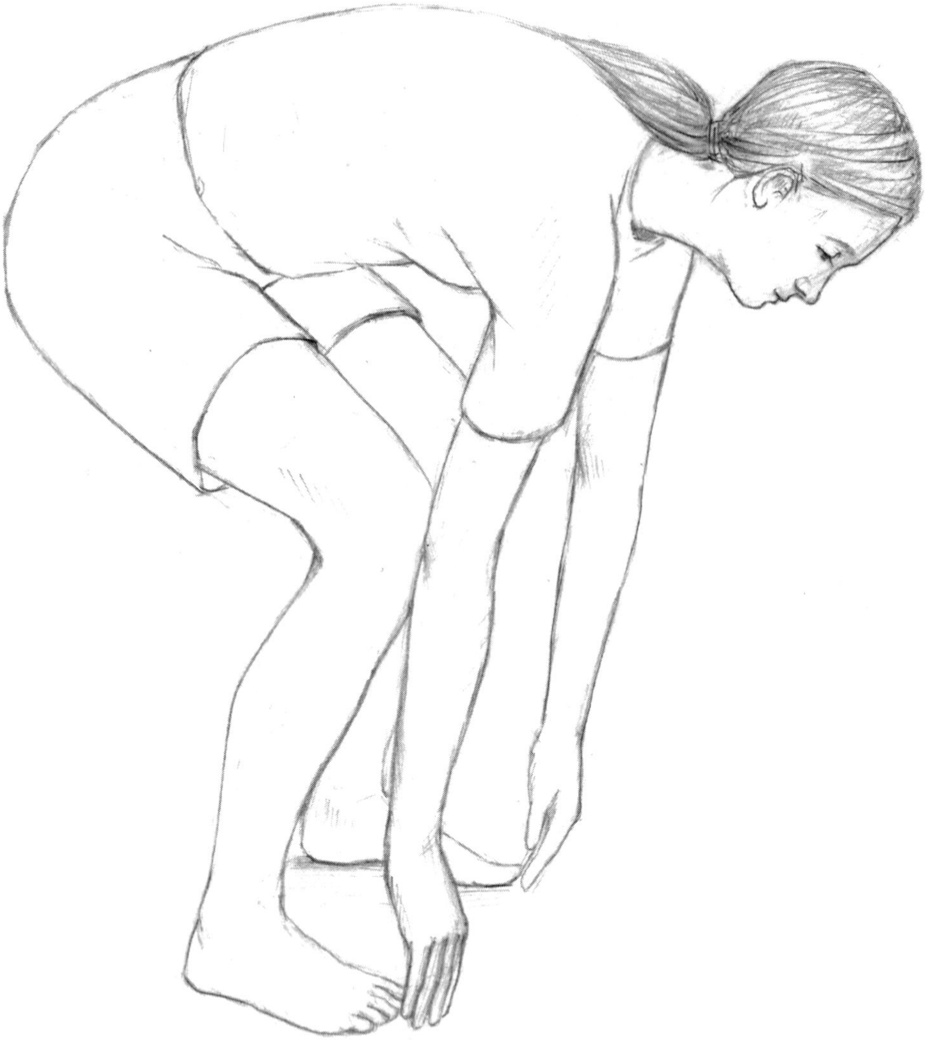

The Racing Dive

Developing your #5 power

Go for—self-encouragement

This is the first full power of the execution phase. Moving from deliberation to liberation, you release and unstintingly throw yourself into action. You encourage yourself to go for your dream. You're willing to take the risk and spring into action. Those who have trouble moving forcefully when the time is ripe often feel indecisive, hesitant—stuck.

Begin development of your #5 power by practicing the following yoga-like exercise.

The 'Racing Dive' Pose

This pose conveys the physical stance and mental attitude of the highly competitive Olympic swimmer whose explosive dive from the starting blocks results in a first-place finish. The head leads and the body completes the action. In this position you get the sense of being on your mark, being set, then springing into action as you go for your goal.

1. Flex your knees and bend forward at the waist.
2. Let your fingers touch your toes.
3. Breathing from your center, hang there for a few moments.
4. Allow the energy and tension to build, as you imagine yourself exploding from the starting block and charging forward toward your goal.
5. Jump forward a few inches, as you conjure up the feeling of making your all-out dive and courageously going full-tilt for your goal.

Other practices/processes/exercises for developing your #5 power:

1. Walk briskly across a field. Punch the air like a prize fighter. Say to yourself—and really believe it: "I am decisive. I take risks. I go for goals. I take the leap. I am courageous.

2. Think of a performance situation in which you tend to hold yourself back. Ask yourself: "Is it worth the risk? Can I handle it if I fail? Are my fears ungrounded?" If your answers are "yes," encourage yourself to go for that goal you've been holding yourself back from. Go out and do it!

3. Take a position on the ground and imagine yourself a sleek black jungle cat. You're not only a survivor, you're a fierce fighter. You hunt for a living. Go into a crouch. Feel yourself springing from a tree and going for your prey.

4. When you experience yourself not going for something that you really want, pause and take a few breaths. Sit down and have a few *imaginary conversations* with people who've been significant in your life—parents, grandparents, teachers, coaches, colleagues, siblings. Discuss with them why you might be holding back from *going for* what you really want. Get their 'permission' to become a go-for-it personality type. Don't stop there. Demand that they support and encourage you in your quest—in your desire to go for your goal.

5. Take a rock-climbing lesson from a certified instructor. As you scale a wall or reach the top of a rock, tell yourself: "This is me. I am the kind of person who has the courage and daring to go for goals and reach the top."

6. Imagine yourself in kindergarten playing a game of musical chairs. As you begin your slow walk around the chairs, envision yourself as the quickest and most energetic kid in the class. You are not passive. You

will not be denied. You always find a way to win. You flex your muscles and sharpen your mental resolve. You *go for* a chair.

7. Play a game of tennis in which you keep running to the net. It's just a practice, so don't be concerned about whether you win or lose the point. Just keep rushing forward. Practice going for it—and getting there.

8. The word *aggressive* is derived from the Latin *ad,* to + *gradi,* to step. Think of an aggressive athlete as a person who vigorously steps forward in pursuit of a goal. Don't hesitate to define your self as *aggressive.* Take steps. *Go for it.*

9. Be inspired by quotations such as these:

> *"Courage is the human virtue that counts most—courage to act on limited knowledge and insufficient evidence. That is all any of us have."*
>
> —Robert Frost

> *"You gain strength, courage, and confidence by every experience in which you really stop to look fear in the face. You must do the thing which you think you cannot do."*
>
> —Eleanor Roosevelt

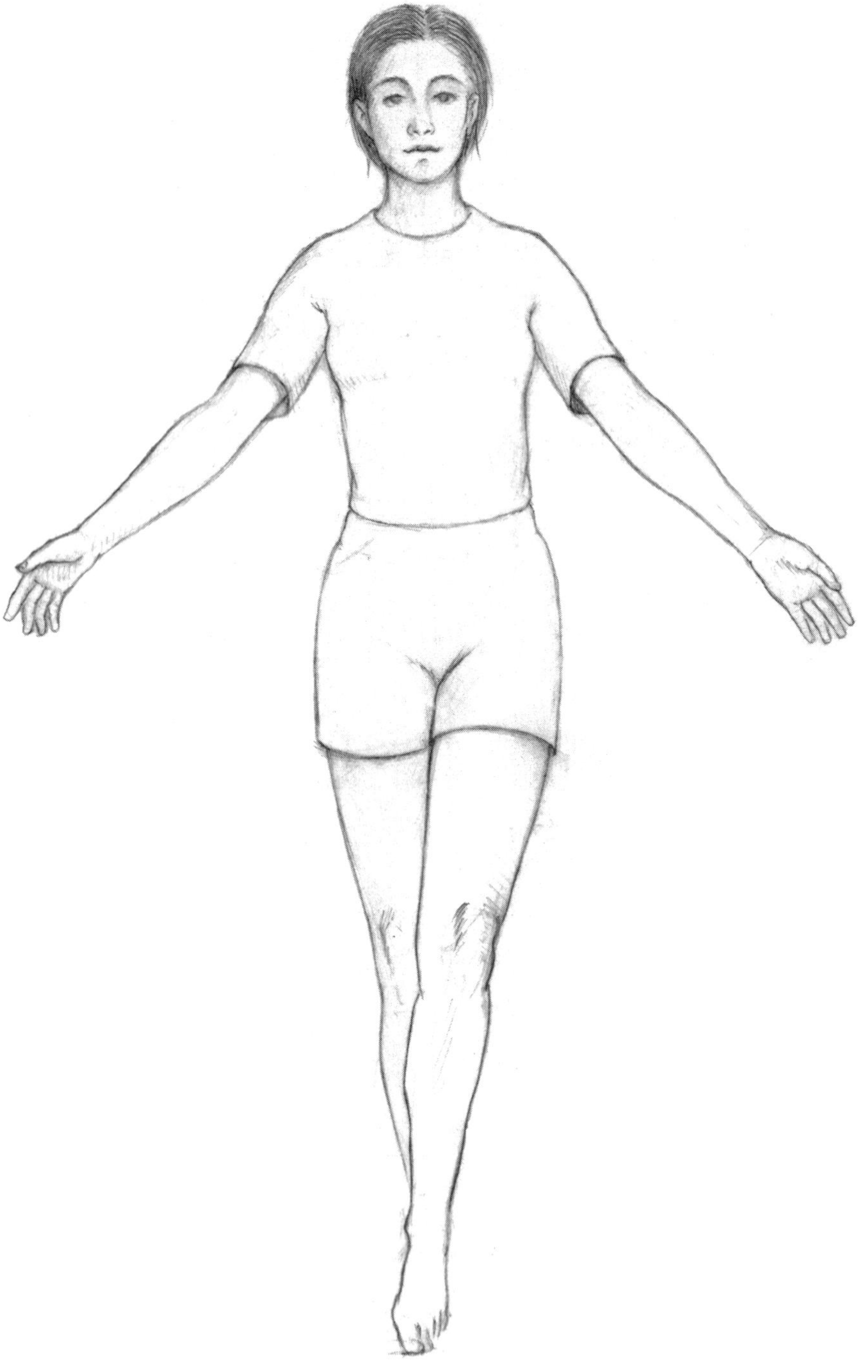

The Tightrope Walker

Developing your #6 power

Focus on—self-discipline

Beyond a decisive commencement of action, goal-oriented activities demand continued attention and energy. The person with a well-developed ability to focus stays on track, never wavering from what he or she is doing. Individuals who need to strengthen their "focus on" capacity are easily distracted. They lack self-discipline. After an initial burst of energy, they may quickly lose their enthusiasm and turn their attention to some other goal. Sustaining attention and effort may feel boring to them.

Practice being focused.

The Tightrope Walker

In this exercise you are forced to coordinate the energies of the body and mind and stay totally focused on doing what you're doing at the time you're doing it. You cannot waver or wobble. From the soles of your feet to the hairs on the top of your head, you must keep your balance and stay on the rope.

1. Stand firmly in place, with one foot directly in front of the other, your arms extended out to your sides.
2. Take a deep breath as you imagine yourself a highly disciplined tightrope walker about to traverse a deep chasm.
3. Slowly and confidently walk the imagined tightrope—best if barefoot.
4. Appreciate the coordination of your body and mind as you're able to maintain your balance and stay focused on the task at hand.
5. With moment-to-moment awareness, walk forward ten feet, then twist and turn, and retrace your steps.

Other practices/processes/exercises for developing your #6 power:

1. There are times to cross streams and wander through the woods. Times to explore and allow the imagination to run wild. But there are also times to practice the art of staying focused and sticking to a chosen path.

   Find a walking stick and a narrow hiking trail of five miles or more. Walk briskly. Stay centered, mindful of where you plant you feet. With each out-breath, let your mantra be: *Stick to the Path…Stick to the Path…Stick to the Path.*

2. Embrace these words and phrases: *undivided attention, focus, staying power, stick-to-itiveness path, discipline.*

3. As you engage yourself in a task with a definite goal, picture yourself as a *harness-horse with blinders.* Stay highly disciplined. Keep your eyes focused straight ahead. Undistracted, stick to your path and speedily pull your chariot to your destination.

4. Take a blank piece of paper and draw a circle in the middle of it about the size of a half-dollar. Now take a sharp pencil and make a dot in the middle of that circle. Hold the pencil a couple millimeters above the dot for a few moments and focus all your attention on what you are doing as you slowly bring the tip of the pencil back down to the dot. Now begin to make little circles expanding outward toward the edge of the circle you just drew. Develop your ability to discipline your mind by keeping your full attention on this meaningless task. Now, convert this admittedly silly exercise into something meaningful. Find something intriguing about keeping all your energy focused on this task.

5. Meditate. Learn how to be comfortable while sitting upright. Keep yourself centered as you breathe in and breathe out.

6. Sit or stand perfectly still. Strike a pose and stick with it. Freeze! Think of yourself as a statue in a park, a street mime, or a mannequin in a department store window. Hold the pose for 30 seconds…then a minute…then 10 minutes. As you keep your body from wavering and wobbling, you'll note how your mind is less inclined to wander. Reflect upon the title of Stanley Kellerman's book on bioenergenic analysis: *Your Body Speaks Its Mind.*

6. Sit! Get yourself centered and comfortable. Clear your mind of all thought. Stay focused on your breathing.

7. Fix your gaze on a lit candle.

   Sit comfortably at a dining room table and from about fifteen inches away, stare intently at the flame of a candle. After holding your gaze for about one minute, deliberately turn your eyes away for a few seconds to some other items in the room. Then quickly bring all of your awareness back to the tiny fire for another minute.

   Repeat this routine about ten times in a row—recognizing your ability to focus totally for a full minute—next discovering how your mind wants to wander a bit—and finally experiencing your capacity to quickly bring yourself back to full attention on a specific item or objective.

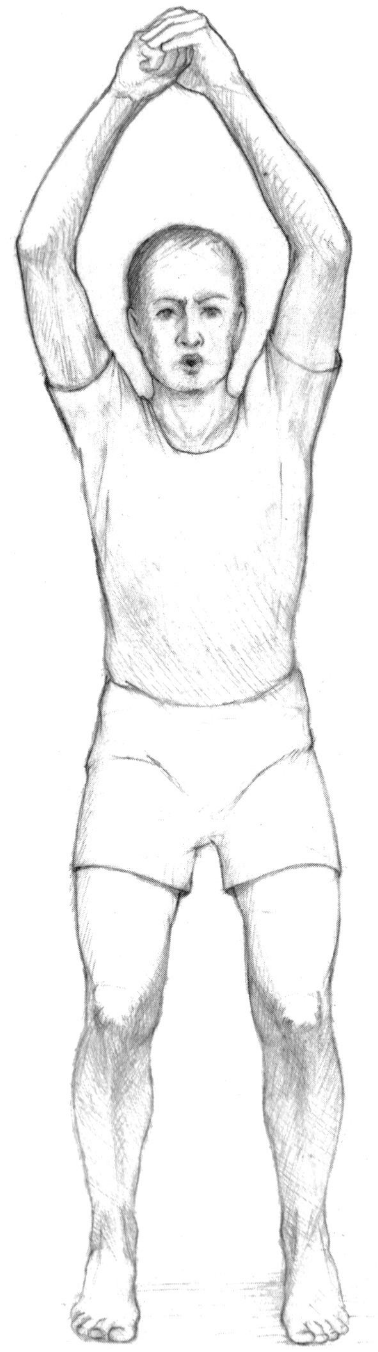

The Hammerer

Developing your #7 power

Breathe out—self-expression

Just as the karate master unleashes her blow with a resounding exhalation, the forceful achiever culminates the thrust of execution with a full release of energy. This total exertion is the natural culmination of the momentum built during the early stages of the act. Individuals who breathe out well hold nothing back and give their all, as they push through any resistance to surmount even the most difficult challenges. They are fully expressive. On the other hand, those who hold back from total exertion often fall just short of achieving their goals. Insufficient breathe-out capacity may also be experienced as a tendency to question the course of action when complete commitment is crucial.

Practice breath work.

The Hammerer

In this exercise imagine that you're playing the carnival game that involves a sledgehammer and a tall pole with a loud bell at the top. Bend your knees, lift the imaginary sledgehammer over your head, and with as much force as you can muster, slam it downward with a full, audible exhalation, propelling the steel ball as high up the post as possible toward that bell. This exercise is a practice in *giving your all.* It is about the total, uninhibited expression of self.

1. Stand comfortably, your feet shoulder-width apart.
2. Bend your knees, inhale deeply, and with your hands clasped together, lift your arms up over your head.
3. On a full and audible exhalation, swing your arms downward swiftly and forcefully, keeping your knees bent throughout the exercise.
4. Come back to an upright position and repeat the exercise several times.
5. Get the sense that your body and mind are in absolute harmony as you give your all to what you're doing.

Other practices/processes/exercises for developing your #7 power:

1. Take a series of karate or kung-fu lessons and ask the instructor for some extra help in coordinating your punches and kicks with good expressive breath work.

2. With an exercise similar to The Hammerer, pretend you're a woodcutter splitting a log. Take a stance, feet about shoulder-width apart, knees slightly bent. With a slow and deliberate inhalation, lift an imaginary ax over your shoulders and head using both hands. With a highly expressive and audible *exhalation,* bring your ax downward and through the "log."

3. Get a court and a basket of tennis balls. Have a player on the opposite side of the net tap nice easy slow shots to you. With a full inhalation on your back-swing, get yourself well-positioned for a full-powered ground stroke, then with a full and audible exhalation, whack the ball swiftly and forcefully over the net. Don't worry about where it goes. Just stay focused on being fully expressive as you stroke the ball.

4. Word play: *self-expression, breathe out, shout, explode.*

5. Practice expressing your emotions. The next time something strikes you as funny, have a good laugh—from your belly. If you're in pain, moan and groan. When you feel sad, have a cry. Let the tears flow.

6. Take singing lessons or join a choral group.

7. Write letters to your friends and family. Share your feelings with them.

8. Get a punching bag. Smack it! Smash it! Whack it! Add sounds to your punches. Puff and pant and let it all out.

9. Practice meditation exercises that focus entirely on the *following of the breath.* Below is an example.

Sit toward the front edge of a chair or meditation cushion with your pelvis tilted forward and your spine straight. Drop your shoulders and seat yourself as comfortably as possible, gently clasping your hands over your belly.

Imagine that three feet in front of you is a large birthday cake with lit candles.

Exhale. Blow out all of the candles. As you pant your way through twenty-five quick and vigorous exhalations, feel the downward and upward movements of your belly.

Now, keeping your hands clasped to your belly, *do* nothing. Simply *be with* each inbreath and each outbreath. Follow your breath for fifteen minutes.

Breathe in through your nose and out through your mouth, feeling your clasped hands rise and fall with the slow and gentle rolling waves of each breath cycle.

Take notice whenever your mind wanders and then gently bring your attention back to your belly and the flow of your breath.

10. Pay attention to your breathing at different times and places during the day. Feel your diaphragm expand and retract a couple times as you inhale and exhale.

The Palm Tree

Developing your #8 power

Ride with—self-surrender

After you've launched a project, there comes a time to allow what you've put into motion to unfold according to the momentum and direction you've set. The white-water kayaker deliberately joins the currents around her. She isn't washed along passively, but neither does she fight the force and flow of the river. Sometimes, your challenge is to yield, to surrender to the forces that are propelling you. If during an endeavor you encounter unanticipated events or input from others, adjust your efforts flexibly while still fundamentally staying your course. Individuals who are poor at "riding with" may interfere with the natural evolution of their projects, because they tend to over-control. To allow any unfolding may feel too passive for them. Partnering with others or accommodating to changing circumstances may be difficult for them, and their undertakings may feel like relentless struggles against opposing forces.

Practice the surrendering of self.

The Palm Tree

In this exercise, imagine you're a young, flexible, well-grounded palm tree. Your strength lies in the fact that you're never uprooted because you know how to stay centered and merge with the elements. You regard a vigorous wind as your friend. You swing and you sway—you yield and surrender—you go with the flow. You ride with it.

1. Stand comfortably, your feet shoulder-width apart.
2. Flex your knees, so they're neither locked nor bent.
3. Breathe slowly and rhythmically.
4. Raise your arms and hands up over your head, and allow your body to sway from side to side and back and forward as if being moved by a swirling wind.
5. Relax the mind.
6. Yield!

Other practices/processes/exercises for developing your #8 power:

1. Word play: *swoosh, glide, flow, coast, partner, merge, let go, harmonious, surrender, ride with.* One by one, embrace these words and phrases. Repeat them to yourself. Think about the essences of these words and their overall feel.

2. Run, walk, or roller-blade down a hill. Just as you reach the bottom, make a quick U-turn and, keeping your rhythm and flow going, head back up that hill and allow the downward momentum that you generated to carry you back to the top. As you reach the top, puffing and panting, do another quick U-turn and let the force of the hill carry you downward. Use that hill. Merge with it. Draw energy from it by surrendering to it.

3. Go white-water rafting. As you navigate your way through treacherous rapids, paddle vigorously to set the right direction and then go with the flow. Be confident that the waters will carry you where you want to go and that you're simply going along for the ride. Let your body and your mind embrace the sensation and exhilaration of coasting, riding, gliding, swishing, swooshing, and zooming down the river.

4. Imagine yourself jumping out of an airplane and skydiving. See yourself going into total free fall. Surrender yourself to the elements with full confidence that your parachute will open and that you will land beautifully, softly, and securely just as you were trained to do. Or, actually do it, if you dare—go skydiving!

5. Take a dance lesson. Learn to waltz. Rent some Fred Astaire videotapes.

6. Recall the fable of the oak tree and the reed. The oak tree, its trunk snapped in half, lies crushed and destroyed by the river bank. He turns to the reed and asks, "How is it that I, so strong and huge, was felled by

the windstorm, while you, weak and frail, survived?" The reed replies, "Rather than resist the force, I surrendered to it."

7. Ride a bike and don't pedal on the downhill slopes. Let your legs fly out to the sides. Fully experience the pull of gravity that allows you to swoosh effortlessly to the bottom of the hill.

8. Learn Tai-chi and Aikido. Experience the power of *yielding to* and *merging with* the energy of outside forces.

9. Discover how to *surrender to the momentum of the act.* Allow it to happen.

Read what Charles Garfield reports on the power of self-surrender:

> *Again and again, athletes have described how at moments of peak performance they felt consumed by the momentum of the event itself, how the activity itself took over, and how they became perfectly synchronized within it.*
>
> *In interviews throughout his career, boxer Ingemar Johansson insisted that his powerful right hand seemed to have a mind of its own, that when the time came to deliver the knockout punch he felt he surrendered to the action rather than taking an active part in it: "Without my telling it to, the right hand goes, and when it hits, there is this good feeling…Something just right has been done."* (Garfield, *Peak Performance)*

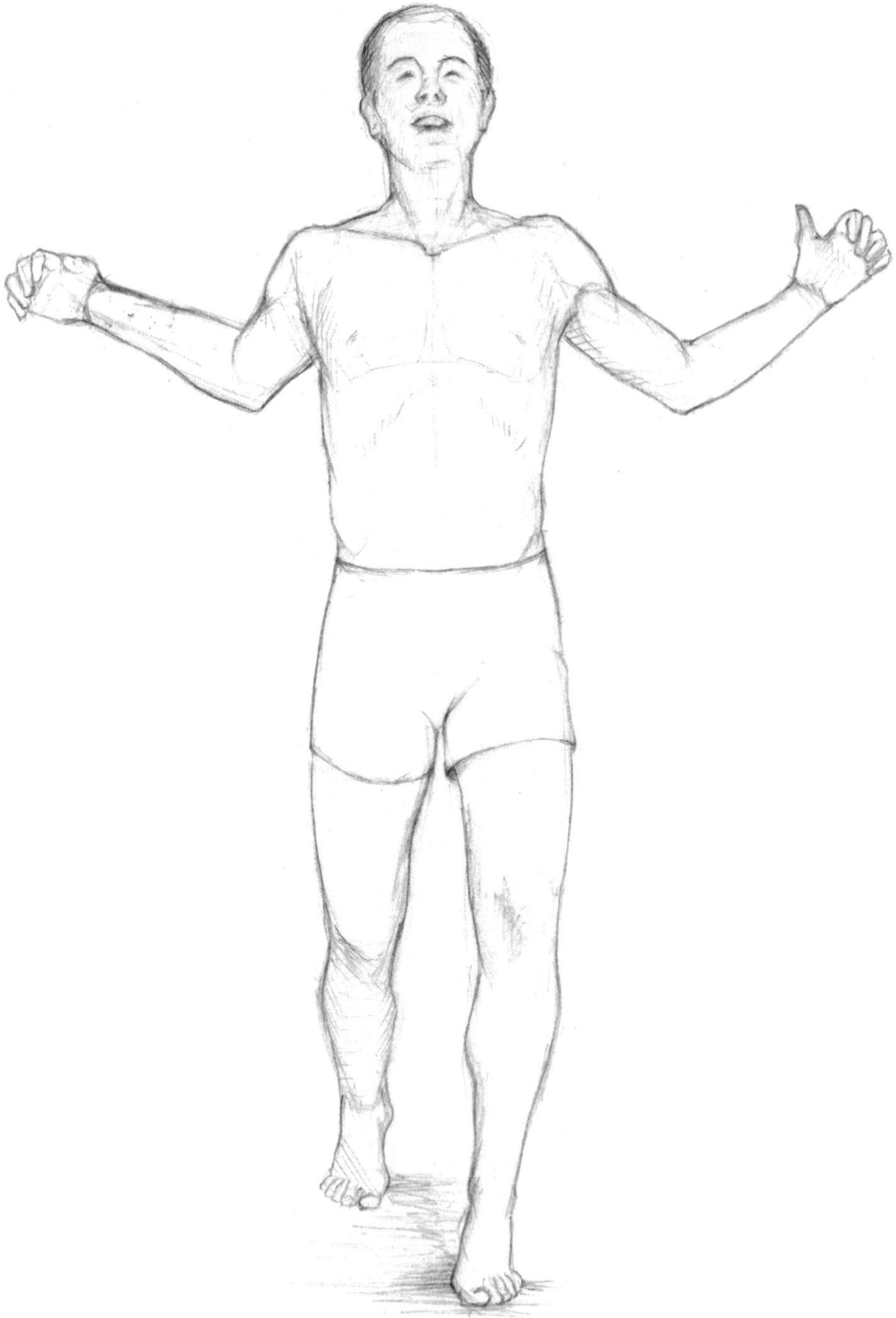

The Finisher

Developing your #9 power

Follow through—self-fulfillment

This is the first full power of the completion phase. Unless you attend faithfully to the finishing touches of an athletic act, you never achieve closure. You must extend the commitment of your energy right on through to the final flourish that completes your achievement. Those who overlook the closing steps or tend to be slipshod in executing them often feel frustrated when their projects fall short of their initial promise. Instead of relishing completions, they may unwittingly avoid them.

Practice your follow-through.

The Finisher

Assume the posture of the fleet-footed sprinter who, with arms extended and chest expanded surges to the finish line, breaks the ribbon, and captures first place. Imagine yourself making that one last, all-out effort to reach your goal and follow through on your commitment to finish what you set out to do.

1 Stand comfortably, feet just a few inches apart.

2. While rising up on your toes, place your right foot forward about 24 inches.

3. On a deep inhalation, stretch out your arms.

4. Throw your shoulders back and thrust out your chest toward an imaginary finish line.

5. As you hold this pose for a few moments, stay with the thought that you're a strong finisher who completes what you start.

6. Repeat the above exercise, stretching the other side of the body by getting up on your toes and placing your *left* foot forward about 24 inches.

Other practices/processes/exercises for developing your #9 power:

1. Make a list of 25 tasks that you started and finished—tasks that you *followed through* on to the end. Say to yourself: *"That's me! I am a strong finisher!"*

2. Imagine yourself a 6'5" superstar on the basketball floor. With the game on the line, you split the seam between two defenders. You lift off, and with both hands on the ball and over the rim, you stuff it. Slam! Dunk! Done! A complete finish. Say to yourself: *"I am a finisher!"*

3. Compose a hand-written letter or note to a special friend or relative. Address the envelope. Seal it. Lick the stamp. Put it in the mailbox. Say to yourself: *"When I start a task, I see it through to the end. I fully complete what I set out to do."*

4. Go through the motions of throwing a baseball. Start with a series of short little tosses. Just half-throws. Flicks of the wrist. Warm-ups. Now place yourself on the mound and do a full wind-up. Make a complete and definitive throw that contains a beginning, a middle, and a clear-cut end with a full follow-through.

5. Get a bucket of golf balls at a driving range and, on your first twenty strokes, deliberately restrain the pivoting of your torso and stop the follow-through of your club about waist high. On your next forty shots, really let loose. Release yourself. Allow your arms to carry forward to the very end of your swing by the full completion of your pivot. In this practice, don't concern yourself about errant flights of the ball. Give yourself a deeply felt sense of a long, smooth, and graceful stroke with a full, flourishing finish that finally comes to rest as the club head gently touches your back. As you complete each full swing of the club, maintain your balance and hold your finish position for a few seconds.

6. Find and read quotations that honor the characteristic of following through on tasks and being a *finisher.*

> *"All endeavor calls for the ability to tramp the last mile,*
> *shape the last plan, endure the last hours toil.*
> *The fight to the finish spirit is the one...characteristic we*
> *must posses if we are to face the future as finishers."*
>
> —Henry David Thoreau

7. Commit yourself to the successful completion of a marathon-like run, swim, bike or hike. Let it be a distance that's not unhealthful, but that's clearly demanding and challenging. Talk to yourself and others about how and why you'll be doing it. Then go out and do it! Experience yourself "walking your talk." Follow through. Fulfill yourself. Completely finish the task you've talked about doing and you've set out to do.

8. Word play: *finished, completed, finality, persistent, done, fulfillment.*

The 'Sit-Up' Exercise

Developing your #10 power

Bounce back—self-trust

After a vicious swing of the bat, the body is fully turned and tightly coiled. But the well-trained athlete trusts his resiliency. He quickly recoils. Whether a hit or a miss, the full extension doesn't result in paralysis or in getting stuck. Moving from the narrow focus of executing the task and fully extending yourself, you spring back from whatever just happened. You face the consequences and *re-center* yourself for your next step.

Practice "bouncing back."

The 'Sit-Up' Exercise

Fundamental to all serious physical exercise programs is the *sit-up*. In addition to strengthening the back muscles and midsection of the body, this exercise expresses a very important mental position, or attitude. When performed slowly and mindfully, the *sit-up* declares in effect: "I can fall flat on my back, but I have the power to get back up again. I can arise. I can bounce back."

1. Lie on your back with your legs flexed and pulled toward your chest.
2. Grasp the undersides of your thighs and rock yourself into a fully upward sitting position.
3. Pause a moment, then allow yourself to fall onto your back again.
4. Repeat this move a dozen times or more with the deeply felt awareness of being flat on your back, then quickly and easily springing upward again.

Other practices/processes/exercises for developing your #10 power:

1. Do a series of ten sit-ups—knees bent, feet on the floor. As you lean back and your head and shoulders touch the floor, say out loud: *"I am down and out, flat on my back!"* Then as you pull yourself upward, say: *"I bounce back, I spring back, I rise again!"*

2. Conjure an image of yourself as one of those inflatable clowns with sand at your base. When you get knocked over, you bounce right back up again.

3. Stand in a doorway and push the backs of your hands against the doorjamb, applying lots of pressure for 15 seconds. Now slowly take a step forward and allow your arms to float upward on their own. Get that sense of your body and mind being up against a wall, then gently rebounding.

4. Internalize these words: *resilient, recovery, resurrection, flexible, buoyant, bounce-back.*

5. Watch live action or videos of accomplished skiers, snowboarders, skateboarders, and figure skaters. Notice how often they fall and how readily they spring back up. When you happen to fall, don't just lie there and feel sorry for yourself. Quickly, nimbly bounce back to your feet and get on with what you're doing. Tell yourself: *"This is the kind of person I am. After a fall, I simply dust myself off and get back up again."*

6. Purchase a high-quality yo-yo, and as you get it to perform well, say to yourself: "This is me. I take a spill and, quick as a whip, I flip right back up again."

7. While keeping your hands flat on a wall, extend your arms and step back a couple feet. Do a series of push-aways. Get the light-hearted feeling

of falling forward, pressing your nose to the wall, then easily springing back to center.

8. Learn judo. Take a class or a few private lessons, and tell the instructor you're particularly interested in learning the art of falling down, then being able quickly to get back up. Recognize that a graceful recovery from a fall has a lot to do with your mental attitude.

9. View a hockey game. Watch how easily the players recover from violent hits. Note how quickly they get back up on their skates after being knocked down. Decide to be this kind of performer. Trust that, after a fall, you'll always be able to get back up on your feet.

10. Keep your sense of humor—realizing that everyone falls and fails from time to time.

> *"Be willing to laugh at yourself. Life really is fun, and so are sports. If you have a particularly disappointing game, find the humor in it. Look for something to laugh about in anything negative that takes place. As one baseball player quipped, 'I was very consistent today—consistently bad!'"*
>
> —Kenneth Baum, *The Mental Edge*

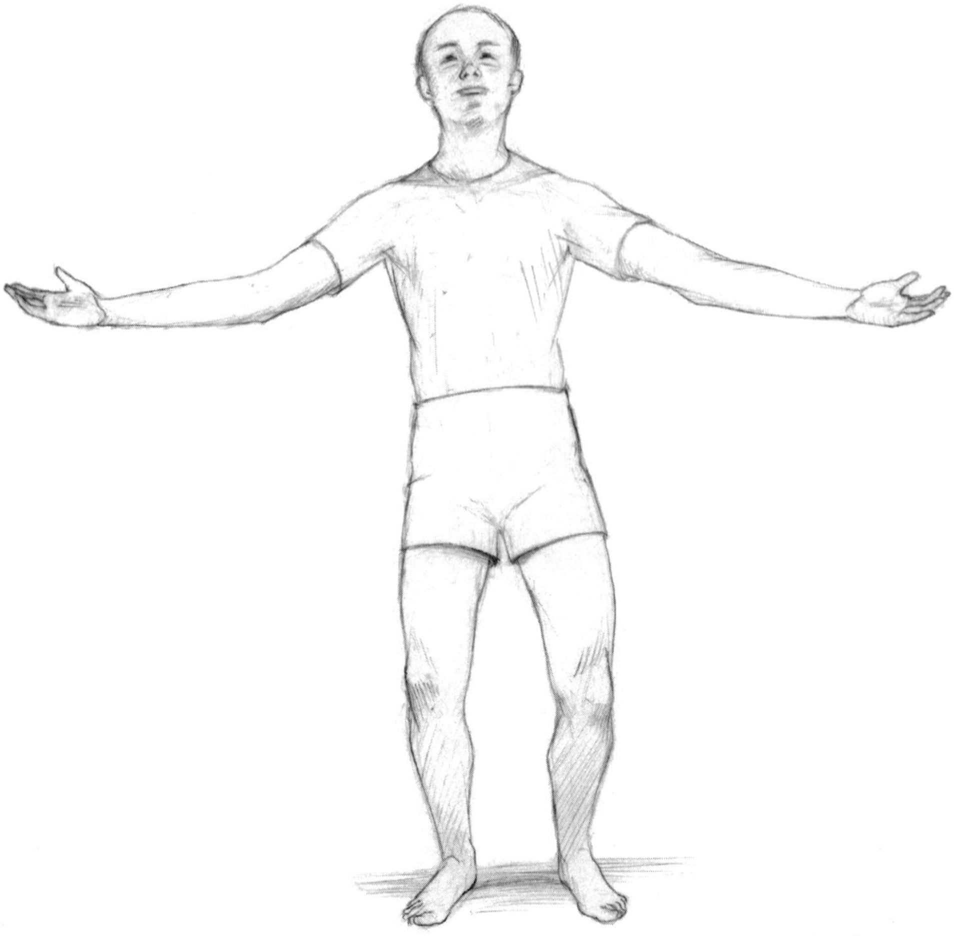

The 'Standing In Awe' Pose

Developing your #11 power

Soak in—self-reflection

Taking time to appreciate and assess what you've done is a crucial part of the completion phase. *Soaking in* involves assimilating and reflecting upon all the feedback available, savoring deeply the successes and fully exploring how and why other outcomes fell short of the mark. The person who soaks in well appreciates both praise and criticism as information that will guide and improve future performance. Failing to soak in fully, a person misses key opportunities to relish accomplishments as well as to learn from them.

Practice self-reflection.

The 'Standing in Awe' Pose

With a deep inhalation, you lean back, spread your arms out wide and embrace your world. Your position says in effect: *"I am open and vulnerable. I stand in reverent wonder—willing and wanting to be judged. I face up to what I just did. Tell me what I need to know."* Then you listen—fully aware and deeply reflective.

1. Assume a comfortable stance, your feet about shoulder-width apart.
2. Rotate your knees outward and curl your toes.
3. Tilt your pelvis forward, lean back, and with a full inhalation, expand the chest and feel the pinching of the blades as you bring your shoulders back.
4. Spread your arms out wide, palms facing forward and up.
5. Tuck the chin (military posture).
6. Reflect. Be mindful.
7. Breathe in…breathe out.

Other practices/processes/exercises for developing your #11 power:

1. Practice being able to judge and evaluate your disappointing acts without being overly harsh or demeaning. Begin with a basic set of questions that will allow you to recall how you did in terms of the Energy Cycle. Ask, for example: "Was I motivated? Was I in control? Did I have a clear sense of direction? Was I disciplined? Did I give my all today?" Simply acknowledge how you performed at a particular moment in time and space.

2. Practice indulging yourself in the afterglow of an act or a job well done. Be your own coach and recognize a self within your Self. Look in the mirror and recognize the performer within you. Say aloud: "*You* are a performer in whom *I*, your Larger Self, am well pleased. *You* did well. *I* did well. *We* all did well."

3. From time to time, practice writing down your achievements. Describe in detail some of the "successful performances" of your day...your week...your month...your year. You don't have to share the writings with anyone else. The benefit lies in reflecting upon what you did.

4. After performing a particular act, such as the stroking of a golf ball, take twenty seconds or more to do a vivid, detailed, *slow-motion instant replay.* See the shot in your mind's eye. Hear yourself doing what you just did. Think of the replay as a video clip that you can now download onto your hard drive. Store it in your memory.

5. In your mind's eye, frequently replay your successful acts. Allow an everyday occurrence to elicit a particular recall. For example, you can make brushing your teeth or combing your hair a "trigger" that sets off a quick replay of one of your achievements.

6. Walk along a crowded street and make a conscious effort to take in all the sounds, scents, and sights. In particular, notice the people. How do they move and gesture? What's their body language? Soak it all in.

7. As a means of improving your skills in the sport of your choice, view professionally developed training videos. Capture the essential moves and actions of the experts. Stock your mind with the "right things" to reflect on.

8. Find and read quotations that will inspire you to learn, grow, develop, examine, improve, evaluate, wonder, reflect. Here are some examples:

"Retire into yourself as much as possible.
Associate with people who are likely to improve you.
Welcome those whom you are capable of improving.
The process is a mutual one. People learn as they teach."

—Seneca

"The unexamined life is not worth living."

—Socrates

"O, happy the soul that saw its own faults."

—Rumi

"People travel to wonder at the height of mountains, at the huge waves of the sea, at the long courses of rivers, at the vast compass of the ocean, at the circular motion of the stars; and they pass by themselves without wondering."

—St. Augustine

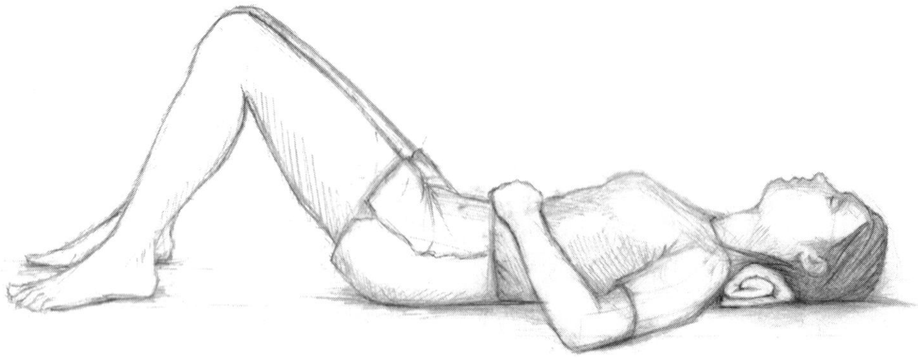

The Sleeper

Developing your #12 power

Power #12 Rest from—self-regeneration

Rest from, the last stage in the completion phase as well as of the entire cycle, can be seen as a kind of punctuation between successive cycles. Performers who are so action-oriented that they have difficulty with even short periods of inactivity are prime candidates for burnout. Over-extension and inadequate rest can have significant negative long-term repercussions on health. Even those individuals who appear to function well without breaks could enjoy improved efficiency, were they to regenerate themselves.

Practice self-regeneration.

The Sleeper

This pose mimics an individual who has fallen into deep slumber. As you lie on your back and close your eyes, it should look to the outside observer that you're sound asleep, breathing deeply and naturally—like a baby. But while your eyes may be closed, you remain wide awake. With moment to moment awareness, you focus all your attention on your breathing—not regulating it in any way, just letting it happen. You merely register the up and down rhythmic sensations of your breathing patterns.

1. Lie on a mat, a carpeted floor, or a firm mattress.
2. Fold a towel into a nice tight roll and place it under the nape of your neck.
3. Tighten your total body: feet, ankles, thighs, chest, arms, cheeks, eyes, forehead.
4. Hold the tightness for 10 seconds. Quickly release.
5. Bend your knees and bring your feet flat to the mat. Clasp your hands over your abdomen and pay attention to its rising and sinking as you pant like a puppy for about half a minute.
6. Now just lie there. Be totally at rest. Don't attempt to regulate your breathing in any manner. Don't do anything. Simply be aware of the rhythmic sensations of your breathing patterns. Act as if you have fallen asleep.

Other practices/processes/exercises for developing your # 12 power:

1. From time to time during the course of your day, get in touch with the rhythm of your breathing and for a few moments allow yourself to just *be where you are.* Don't impose your will or expect anything from the self. Just observe. Stare out the window. Gaze at a bird. Be patient and still as you stand in line. Practice being passive. Be aware of your *non-doing.*

2. Seek out quiet and aesthetically pleasing places where you can sit and contemplate. One of these spots should be within your own home. But within a seven-mile radius of where you live, find at least seven other peaceful places, (e.g. on the bank of a river, on a hillside near a tree in a park, in a church, a temple, or a museum). Designate these places as your own special rest spots and frequent them often.

3. Shake! Shimmer! Then let the body relax and come to rest. *"With your arms hanging loosely at your sides, begin by shaking your hands. Then let the vigorous vibration move up to include your arms and then your shoulders. Feel both arms vibrate energetically and rapidly. Then let the shaking slowly subside and feel the tingling throughout your body. Now loosely shake one leg—then the other."* (Sobel, D.S., *To Your Health.)*

4. Lie down and tense your entire body. Bend back your ankles. Clench your stomach muscles. Stiffen your neck. Furrow your brow. Hold the tension for a few seconds, then quickly relax. Repeat the tense/relax sequence 3 or 4 times. Then flop onto a couch or a bean-bag chair or lean way back in a La-Z-Boy chair. Go limp. Just be there, loose and easy, like a rag doll.

5. Lie down and get yourself perfectly comfortable. Picture yourself sunbathing on a nice warm day. As you imagine yourself looking up at a clear blue sky, you may occasionally find that some unwanted thoughts and images come to mind. Don't fight them. Just view them as a scattering

of clouds that will soon drift away. Wait for them to disappear as you refocus your mind on the natural rhythm and flow of your breathing.

6. Take a bath. Lie quietly in the deep water. Stretch your muscles and massage the kinks. Clasp your hands over your abdomen and feel your belly rise and fall with the rhythm of your breathing. Luxuriate in the warmth. Rest.

7. Get massages. And massage yourself. *"Lying on your bed, close your eyes. Put both hands lightly over your face and with your middle fingers stroke your forehead gently in light circular movements, all the way up to the temples. Repeat each of these movements a few times, until you feel relaxed and ready to drop off to sleep."* (Motter and Savary, *The Sleep Book*.)

8. Honor *rest.* Consider it productive.

"Take rest; a field that has rested gives a bountiful crop."

—Ovid

"Rest when you're weary. Refresh and renew yourself, your body, your mind, your spirit. Then get back to work."

—Hedley Ralph Marston

●●●●●●●●●●●●●●

The 12 Powers defined in this chapter are not superficial tricks or strategies for the playing field. Rather, these powers are essential capacities for performing maximally in any arena. An underdeveloped power of the Energy Cycle can be thought of as an 'energy block' or 'stuck point' that keeps you from performing at your best. Mindful practice is the prescription. One by one you can heighten your awareness of an individual power and seek to strengthen that particular capacity. Eventually you will develop and integrate all 12 Powers and be able to access them spontaneously.

11

CYCLE YOUR ENERGIES

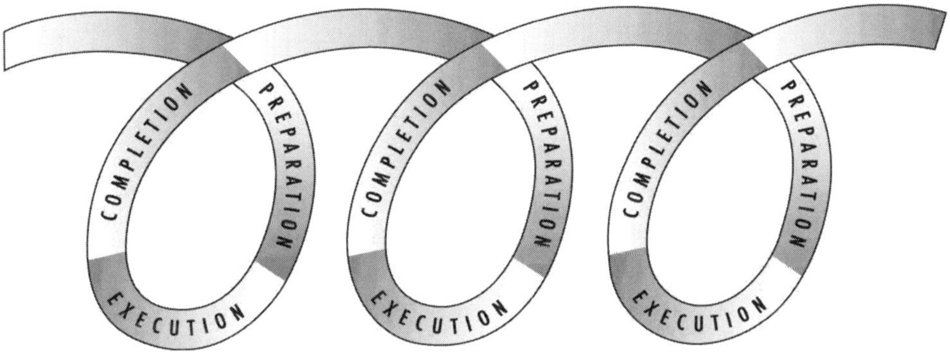

Norbert Wiener's task was to build a machine that could hit a moving target.

It was the beginning of World War II, and the Harvard professor's target was enemy aircraft. His machine would be required to receive data from aircraft-tracking radar, predict the future flight course of planes, and accurately aim anti-aircraft guns.

In working on the practical problems of war, Wiener and his colleagues developed a new theory of how systems work, which he called cybernetics. He quickly realized that the problem he was trying to solve—how to adjust actions to accommodate an ever-changing situation in the real world—was as crucial to the understanding of human behavior as it was to the designing of complex machines.

In the half-century since Wiener first described his theory of cybernetics, his ideas have been applied to such varied tasks as the design of computers, the development of artificial intelligence, and a greater understanding of how the human brain controls conscious activities.

The term cybernetics is taken from the Greek for "steersman," and a cybernetic system is one that, through the analysis of environmental information, is able to set the direction for a course of action.

One of the simplest examples of a cybernetic system is the common thermostat, which can be programmed to maintain a pre-determined temperature inside the home. The thermostat's sensors determine when the temperature has dropped below the desired level, then sends a message to the furnace to warm up the house. When the temperature reaches the desired level, the thermostat again signals the furnace, this time to shut off.

The sophistication of today's cybernetic systems far exceeds the complexity of the thermostat. Computerized robots now use television cameras and advanced sensors to "see," "feel," and "hear" what goes on around them and to adjust their responses to carry out complex tasks. Spacecraft have explored our solar system. Computers control the environments of entire buildings, the flow of oil through pipelines, and the performance of our cars' engines.

In the comparison of machines and humans, the human brain is the "control center" that receives feedback information from the environment through the five senses. The control center processes that information and instructs the body on what actions it should take. The entire cybernetic system is completed—the loop is closed—when the environment is altered by the actions of the body, producing new feedback signals that the senses relay to the brain.

The inner workings of the human brain—the control center of the human cybernetic system—have revealed themselves slowly. The Energy Cycle provides a peek into that control center. In so doing, it offers a way of decoding the achievement process and refining the way we process information and adapt our actions in the real world. Indeed, the Energy Cycle itself is a cybernetic system, one that steers us on the course of successful action and the attainment of goals.

Consider the mental processing of the highly effective golfer as he locates the ball that he has hit onto the fairway; estimates his distance to the green; tosses a few blades of grass into the air to determine the direction and strength of the wind; selects the appropriate club from his bag; completes his swing with just the right velocity; watches as the ball starts off to the left, sails high, and then, moved by the breeze, drifts rightward, landing on the green and rolling to within a few feet of the pin.

How did the golfer cause all this to happen? One might say that is was through the art and science of cybernetics. More precisely, the golfer got it to happen through his use of a very specific cybernetic system—the Energy Cycle.

In the *preparation* phase of the cycle, the mind processes key information, setting a course of action by matching the facts of the environment against the individual's goals and aspirations. In the *execution* phase, that action is carried out, pushing the individual onward toward his goals and altering his world. In the *completion* phase, the mind accepts and assimilates feedback about the impact of the act, measuring its effectiveness.

With the completed loop of this cybernetic system, the individual is ready for a new cycle. With each success, the spiraling process advances the individual ever closer to his ultimate destination.

Because the process of energy cycling keeps us perpetually in contact with our environment, we stay in the moment and don't become overly concerned about ultimate achievements. We are able to remain in harmony with the world around us as we improve our ability to act in that world. And with each successful act or cycle, our goals are revisited, revised, and refined. Like Norbert Wiener, we are trying to hit a moving target—our own aspirations for optimal performance and for success in the world around us.

●●●●●●●●●●●●●

Louis Couffignal, one of the pioneers of cybernetics, defined it as "the art of assuring efficiency of action." *The mystery of how to perform at your best is solved: It is a matter of acquiring the 13th Power (mastery of the Energy Cycle) and applying the principles of cybernetics to your everyday acts.*

Ending

> *"People say that what we're all seeking is a meaning for life. I don't think that's what we're really seeking. I think that what we're seeking is an experience of being alive, so that our life experiences on the purely physical plane will have resonances within our own innermost being and reality, so that we actually feel the rapture of being alive..."*
>
> —Joseph Campbell

This book exhorts you to *perform at your best.* While most of us are intrinsically motivated to do so, understanding the nature of your particular reasons for wanting to succeed will strengthen both your resolve and your abilities.

Perhaps your investment in performing optimally is merely an extension of your core values: you are achievement-oriented; you pursue excellence; you like to win. Or maybe it's because you embrace sport as yoga or as a martial art and discover that performing at your best enables you to focus the mind and develop additional emotional and physical strength. Or maybe optimal performance serves mainly as an adventure in moment-to-moment awareness—a way to practice mindfulness and be intensely active while remaining calm and at peace.

Whatever their motivations, in my view there's one main reason why people frequently fail to maximize their energies and maintain their desire to perform optimally. It's this: the experience just isn't intrinsically pleasurable enough. It's perceived as being too stressful, too much of an effort; it's experienced as burdensome and just not enough fun.

The 13th Power solves that problem. When you master both the *self* and the Energy Cycle, you dramatically increase your chances of experiencing the profound joy of simply doing what you are doing. You welcome the stress because you're confident you can manage it and, knowing your performance itself carries an intrinsic reward, you're no longer overly concerned about capturing an external prize.

Mastery of the 12 powers enables mastery of the *preparation, execution*, and *completion* phases of your act. You are able to "cycle your energies." By this I mean your capacity to string together a series of successful acts or "spirals" wherein and whereby you fire up, settle yourself down, and go for your goal with confidence—followed by a period of recovery, before starting the cycle all over again and taking on another challenge, another act. You discover the proper rhythm and pulse, and you get on a roll—your activity becomes a delicious cycle. You're in the moment. You don't consciously think about activating your 12 energies. It simply happens. You've developed your powers and now you unconsciously access them. Integration and mastery of your 12 energies is your 13th Power and becomes who you are—your characteristic style of acting and reacting.

The concept of energy cycling is referred to by sport psychologist, James Loehr, as "making waves." I like the way he says it:

> *Making waves means making cycles—cycles of stress and recovery. The more the better. The higher the better. We need to oscillate, move, change. We need to make waves, lots of waves—mental, physical, emotional. The opposite of wave-making is linearity. The more linear we become in our lives, the less productive, less happy, and less healthy we will be. All stress without recovery becomes linear, and all recovery without stress becomes linear. To get the most out of life we must pulsate, oscillate, and vibrate.*
>
> —*Toughness Training for Life*

Pulsating, oscillating, vibrating—it's not only healthful, it's fun. It tickles and tingles.

Sport can be trivial amusement. But it can also be a path—a way of awareness—a journey toward self-discovery and self-development. Fill your sport, as well as your whole life, with exhilarating periods of activity and intensity, followed by serene periods of rest, recovery, and re-creation.

So, no more excuses. Go out and live that kind of life. You now know how to gain mastery of the self. You know how to integrate body and mind. You know how to heighten your awareness in action. You know how to give flight to your soul.

Neither in sports nor in the game of life can you expect *all* of your acts to be "winning plays." But if you access your 13th Power (energy mastery) you'll perform at your best, enjoy the experience, and dramatically increase your chances of achieving desired outcomes.

Awaken your self. Stay wholeheartedly involved in doing what you're doing. Enjoy every moment. Energize. Capture the rapture of being alive.

References and Recommended Readings

Benson, Hebert. *The Relaxation Response*. New York: William Morrow, 1975.

Campbell, Joseph, with Bill Moyers. *The Power of Myth*. New York: Doubleday, 1988.

Cooper, Andrew, *Playing in the Zone*. Boston & London: Shambhala, 1998.

Csikszentmihalyi, Mihalyi. *Flow: The Psychology of Optimal Experience*. New York: Harper & Row, 1990.

Dreyer, Danny, with Dreyer, Katherine. *Chi Running: A Revolutionary Approach to Effortless, Injury-Free Running*. New York: Simon & Schuster, 2004.

Gallwey, Timothy W. *The Inner Game of Tennis*. New York: Random House, 1974.

Garfield, Charles, *Peak Performance: Mental Training Techniques of the World's Greatest Athletes*. Los Angeles: Jeremy P. Tarcher, Inc., 1984.

Giamatti, A. Bartlett. *Take Time for Paradise: Americans and Their Games*. New York: Crossroad, 1984.

Jackson, Phil. *Sacred Hoops*. New York: Hyperion, 1995

Kabat-Zinn, Jon. *Wherever You Go, There You Are*. New York: Hyperion, 1994.

King, Billie Jean, with Chapin, Kim. *Billie Jean*. New York: Harper & Row, 1974.

Leonard, George. *The Silent Pulse*. New York: EP. Dutton, 1978.

Loehr, Jim, and Schwartz, Tony. *The Power of Full Engagement*. New York: The Free Press, 2003.

Mack, Gary, with David Casstevens. *Mind Gym*. New York: McGraw-Hill, 2001.

Morehouse, Laurence E. *Maximum Performance*. New York: Simon & Schuster, 1977.

Murphy, Michael, and White, Rhea A. *The Psychic Side of Sports*. Reading, Mass.: Addison-Wesley Publishing, 1978.

Nicklaus, Jack. *Golf My Way*. New York: Simon and Schuster, 1974.

Parent, Joseph. *Zen Golf: Mastering the Mental Game*. New York: Doubleday, 2000.

Russell, Bill, and Branch, Tony. *Second Wind: The Memoirs of an Opinionated Man*. New York: Random House. 1979.

Will, George F., *Men at Work: The Craft of Baseball*. New York: Macmillan Publishing Company.1990.

About the Author

A. Alex Wortman is an inventor, entrepreneur, performance coach, and speaker who has consulted with schools, corporations, and other organizations for more than twenty-five years. He has worked extensively in the broad areas of sports psychology and human resource development.

As a workshop leader, Alex has attracted a wide audience with his model for self-mastery and personal improvement. Drawing upon traditional Western psychology, Eastern philosophy, meditation practices and the martial arts, Alex leads participants to "personal best" performances in areas ranging from sports and the performing arts to business.

With his interest in building better learning environments, Alex—in partnership with his wife, Zena Sheinberg—founded the Glancer Corporation in 1986 and created and patented the gutter deflection devices that spawned the "bumper bowling" craze. Their patented products, now marketed by the Brunswick Corporation have become a worldwide industry standard. The invention and their psychology for skill-development were featured on the Connie Chung Show (CBS) and in numerous publications, including *The Chicago Tribune*, *The Detroit Free Press*, and *People* magazine.

Alex is a licensed psychotherapist. His postgraduate studies were at Wayne State University and the University of Michigan.

The author lives in Ann Arbor, Michigan.

13TH POWER

TRAINING AND DEVELOPMENT

WITH

A. ALEX WORTMAN & ASSOCIATES

For information on speaking engagements and consulting, and for customized training for individuals and groups in conjunction with professionals in golf, tennis, and other sports, please contact us at:

www.performingatyourbest.com

Address: 1705 Wells Street
Ann Arbor, Michigan 48104

E-mail: Wortman@comcast.net gmail.com

Telephone: (734) 665-6580 478-0044